crochet FOR kids

crochet FOR kids

Basic Techniques
& Great Projects
that Kids Can Make
Themselves

Franziska Heidenreich

STACKPOLE
BOOKS

Contents

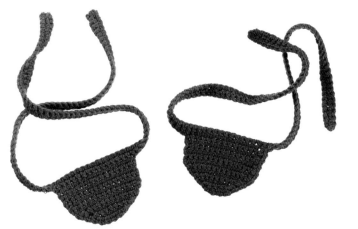

Easy as ABC

Have you ever seen a great homemade hat, a beautiful crocheted scarf, or a little funny accessory made from yarn and asked yourself: How do you actually do that? With this book, you can learn how to crochet easily, even if you've never held a crochet hook in your hand before. Bracelets, leg warmers, a scarf, a purse, cool hacky-sacks, pirate mustaches, a stuffed cat—with the help of detailed and easy-to-understand instructions, you can crochet all these projects and more, as easy as A-B-C! First, read the chapters in the introduction on tools, yarn, and basic crochet techniques, and you'll know everything you need to get started!

The projects in this book are organized according to their difficulty. Start with the easier ones at the beginning and then work up to the projects for pros at the end. The more practice you have, the more things you can try out—even designing your own creations. All the projects call for specific colors, but you can change any of them to make each project in your favorite colors.

Here we go! Get out your crochet hook and yarn and get started. You will soon be making awesome accessories and gifts. You can become a true crochet pro with this book!

I hope you have a lot of fun!

Franziska Heidenreich

Crochet for Kids

What are chain stitches? How do you do a double crochet? Why do you need a magic loop?

This chapter will teach you everything that you need to know about crochet tools, the various types of yarn, and the different crochet techniques.

Have fun!

A Short Guide to Yarn

There are many different types of yarn made from various materials with lots of different characteristics. Some yarns are spun from natural materials such as the wool of sheep, alpacas, or other animals; others are made from plant fibers, such as cotton. Synthetic yarns are made from man-made fibers. Many yarns are a mixture of both natural and synthetic materials.

A Few Kinds of Yarn

Yarn from Plant Fibers

Cotton yarn is smooth and very clearly shows the structure of the crochet stitches. It is available in many different colors and thicknesses. People usually crochet pot holders or summer clothes from cotton since the yarn feels cool on the skin. There are also yarns made of bamboo, flax, and other plant fibers.

Yarn from Animal Hair

Yarn made from wool or other animal hair is fuzzier than other yarns. It will keep you quite warm, which is why jackets, sweaters, and socks are usually knit from wool yarn. But sometimes pure wool feels a bit scratchy on the skin. There are some special softer kinds of wool yarn: merino or lopi wool comes from sheep, mohair or cashmere yarn is from goats, alpaca is from (you guessed it!) alpacas, and angora yarn is from rabbits.

Yarn from Man-Made Fibers

Acrylic is the most common kind of synthetic yarn; others include polyester and nylon. These kinds of yarn can have very different appearances. When they are processed into microfibers, they are very smooth and fine. Yarns made from man-made fibers are usually not scratchy, but they are somewhat less stable when it comes to their shape and quickly form little nubs on the surface when you wear them (this is called "pilling"). Acrylic yarn is available in an unbelievable variety of colors and thicknesses. And it is relatively inexpensive.

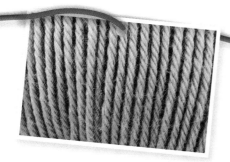

Wool Blends

Many yarns are a mixture of different types of fiber, such as wool and acrylic. The mixture of these two materials results in a yarn that is warm but not scratchy, does not pill so quickly, and is inexpensive. It is usually very easy to work with this kind of yarn.

Novelty Yarn

Some yarns have silver threads (such as lurex) or stretchy materials (such as spandex) spun into them. These are called novelty yarns. In addition, there are loopy yarns, fuzzy yarns (often called "eyelash yarn"), and even yarn with pom-poms or ruffles. It is usually better to use a big crochet hook to work with these special yarns to show them off in the best way.

Yarn Colors

Yarn is available in every imaginable color variation. Many yarns are single-colored, but there are also multicolored yarns. In tweed yarn, the fibers that are twisted with each other have different colors. In variegated yarn, the entire strand of yarn changes color as you go along.

TIP

Instead of just using yarn, you can crochet with anything that is a long strand—which includes twine, jewelry wire, string, strips of plastic bag, and ribbon. Maybe you have some ideas of your own. Just try it out!

What Do the Labels Tell You?

Everything you need to know about your yarn is on the label (the paper ribbon glued around the skein of yarn).

Net Wt • Poids net • Peso Neto
50 g / 1.75 oz

Approx / Approx / Aprox
125 m / 136 yds / vgs / yds

The amount of yarn is given in two ways: The weight of the skein is usually in grams (g) or ounces (oz.). The length, given in yarns (yd.) or meters (m), lets you know how long the yarn will be when you unwrap it from the ball.

The yarn labels always say which company made the yarn (on this label, it's Patons) and the name of the yarn (Grace).

100% Mercerized Cotton
100% Coton mercerisé
100% Algodón mercerizado

The label will also tell you what kind of fiber the yarn is made from—cotton, wool, acrylic, bamboo, etc.

The yarn weight symbol tells you how thick the strand of yarn is. Yarns go from 0, Lace weight (the thinnest yarn of all), to 6, Super Bulky (the thickest yarn of all). Pay attention to the weight of yarn called for in each project and make sure to use yarn from the same weight category.

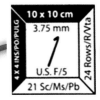

This symbol tells you a lot of things. In the center, it has the size of crochet hook that the yarn company recommends for this kind of yarn—size F-5 (3.75 mm). You don't have to use this exact size, but something close to it will probably work best.

This symbol also tells you about the gauge—how many stitches or rows in an inch—the yarn will give you. This one tells you that with a size F hook, you will get about 21 single crochets side-to-side and 24 rows of single crochet in a 4- by 4-in. (10- by 10-cm) square. You can use this information to figure out if the yarn will work well for your project.

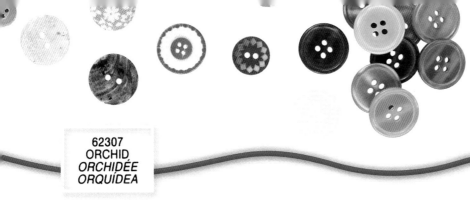

62307
ORCHID
ORCHIDÉE
ORQUÍDEA

Most yarn labels will say the color name, or color number—or both. This is good information to save in case you run out of yarn and need to buy more of the same color.

Sometimes yarn labels will have another number for the color, the dye lot number. This number tells you what batch of dye the skein came from. Even when the color name is the same, different batches of dye may come out just a little bit different. So if the yarn you use has a dye lot number on it, you should try to get skeins from the same dye lot so that they'll match.

TIP

Medium-weight yarn (weight category 3, 4, or 5) is usually a good choice for beginners. It can be hard to see the stitches with very thin yarn.

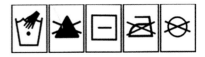

These symbols tell you how to take care of your project after it's finished. There are a lot of symbols for different instructions; the ones here, from left to right, mean "hand-wash in cold water," "do not bleach," "dry flat," "do not iron," and "do not dry clean."

TIP

You could start a yarn notebook to remember the details about yarn you have used. Save one label from each kind of yarn you try, together with a sample of each color you used and the color numbers or names. This way, you will always have the care instructions for your crocheted items, as well as the information about the colors you used—just in case you want to buy more.

Basic Equipment

Tools

Crochet Hooks

You can buy crochet hooks in various sizes and different materials, with or without plastic or rubber grips. Metal crochet hooks with a soft grip are the best to start out with. The size of the crochet hook usually has a letter and a number, plus another number that tells the hook's diameter in millimeters. This book uses hooks in sizes from C-2 (2.75 mm) to L-11 (8 mm).

Yarn Needles

Yarn needles, also called tapestry needles, have a rounded tip and a large eye. This is why they are good to use for sewing with yarn. The round tip lets you go through the loops of stitches without accidentally getting stuck in the fibers of the yarn.

Sewing Needles

You can use sewing needles to attach little buttons and beads to crocheted projects since yarn needles do not fit into their holes.

Safety Pins

You can use a safety pin to secure the last loop that you worked while you do something else (such as stuff the project with fiberfill). You can also use it to secure strands of chain stitches while you test their length.

Pins

You can use pins to hold the individual parts of your crochet project together while you sew them.

Scissors

Cut off threads with a little sharp pair of scissors. The sharper the scissors, the smoother the cut will be—making it easier to thread a needle for sewing.

Stitch Marker

You can use the stitch marker to mark the beginning or end of a round, for example. Another method is to tuck a little scrap of yarn of a different color into your work and then simply pull it out at the end.

Fabric Glue Stick

You can glue together the crochet pieces that you do not want to sew. A regular glue stick will not work for this—you need one specially made for gluing fabric.

Other Materials

Hair Bands

For little pieces that are going to be made into hair accessories, you'll need elastic hair bands to attach them to. These are available in many bright colors, so it is usually easy to find one to match your project.

Buttons and Beads

Buttons and beads are great for decorating projects. A few beads can pep up even a very simple crochet project. You can buy buttons and beads in a variety of colors and sizes. You can also take buttons off of old pieces of clothing and reuse them.

Rice, Dried Beans, or Cherry Pits

Rice, small dried beans (such as lentils), or cherry pits (clean, dry ones) are good filling materials for door-stoppers, hacky-sacks, and beanbag animals. Remember that you cannot wash projects that are filled with these, and if you fill something with rice, the stitches must be very tight, since otherwise the grains will slip through them. You can use an item filled with rice, beans, or pits as a heating pad if you put it in the oven or microwave for a short time. You can also get plastic beans that you can use to fill projects; you can wash projects filled with these plastic pellets, but do not microwave them.

Ribbons

Satin or chiffon ribbons are used for some of the projects. These ribbons are available in many different colors and patterns.

Fiberfill

Fiberfill is used to stuff pillows, crocheted animals, and dolls. When you buy it, make sure that it can be washed. Always stuff your project a little bit at a time. This makes it easier to get the stuffing into the shape you want.

Iron-On Patches or Fusible Web

You can iron your crocheted motifs onto T-shirts or other pieces of clothing with iron-on patches or fusible web. When working with these products, be sure to always pay attention to the manufacturer's instructions.

Crocheting Step by Step

Starting Loop

Unwind about 6 in. (15 cm) of yarn from the ball and tie it into an adjustable loop as shown here. This kind of loop is called a slip knot.

Holding the Hook and Yarn

1 Take the crochet hook in your right hand (for lefties: left hand) and insert it, from right to left (lefties: left to right), through the starting loop. Pull on the end of the yarn with the other hand so that the loop tightens around the crochet hook.

2 Bring the end of the yarn attached to the ball (this is called the working yarn) over your left index finger (lefties: right index finger), about 4 in. (10 cm) away from the hook.

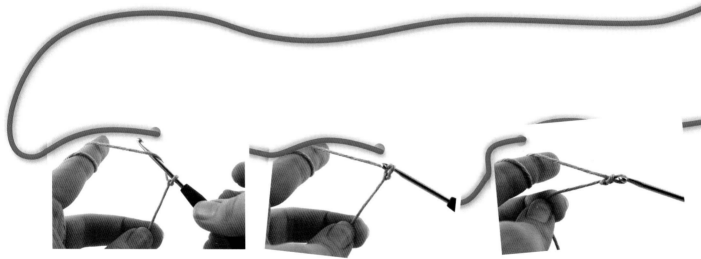

Chain Stitch

1 Start with the crochet hook in the starting loop.

2 With the hook pointing upward, bring the hook under and up against the working yarn, so that the yarn is wrapped over the top of the hook. This step is called "yarn over."

3 Pull the crochet hook back, turning it while you do this so that the hook points downward. Pull the yarn you caught through the starting loop. One chain stitch is done.

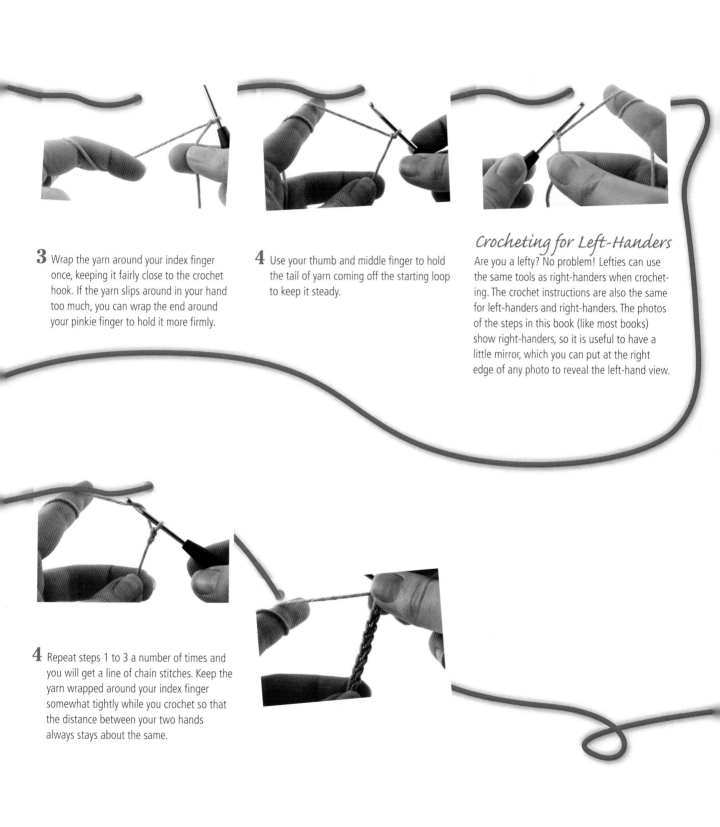

3 Wrap the yarn around your index finger once, keeping it fairly close to the crochet hook. If the yarn slips around in your hand too much, you can wrap the end around your pinkie finger to hold it more firmly.

4 Use your thumb and middle finger to hold the tail of yarn coming off the starting loop to keep it steady.

Crocheting for Left-Handers

Are you a lefty? No problem! Lefties can use the same tools as right-handers when crocheting. The crochet instructions are also the same for left-handers and right-handers. The photos of the steps in this book (like most books) show right-handers, so it is useful to have a little mirror, which you can put at the right edge of any photo to reveal the left-hand view.

4 Repeat steps 1 to 3 a number of times and you will get a line of chain stitches. Keep the yarn wrapped around your index finger somewhat tightly while you crochet so that the distance between your two hands always stays about the same.

Single Crochet

1 Start with a slip knot and crochet a row of chain stitches. Then crochet one more chain stitch—this is called the "turning chain." But don't turn your work at this point.

2 Insert the crochet hook into the second chain stitch from the hook. You will have two strands of yarn above the hook and one strand of yarn below the crochet hook.

3 Now point the tip of the crochet hook upward and yarn over (wrap the working yarn around the hook). Use the hook to pull the yarn back through the chain stitch.

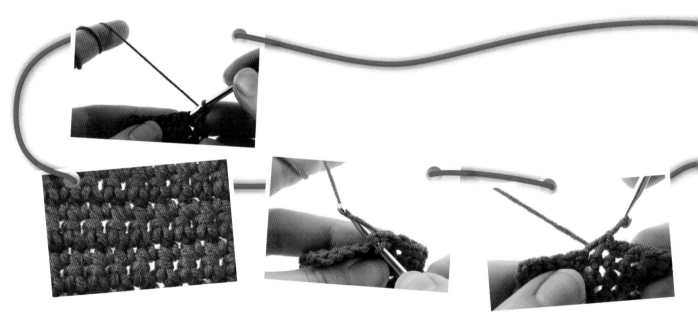

5 Repeat steps 2 to 4 until you are at the end of the row. To work another row of single crochet, make 1 chain stitch for the turning chain, turn the piece around, and work back across the row in the same way.

Slip Stitch

Slip stitches are very short stitches sometimes used to join parts of a piece together. To make a slip stitch, insert the hook into the stitch and pull up a loop just like for single crochet. But don't stop there and yarn over again—continue to pull the loop you pulled up through the stitch so that you pull it through the loop that is on your crochet hook in the same movement.

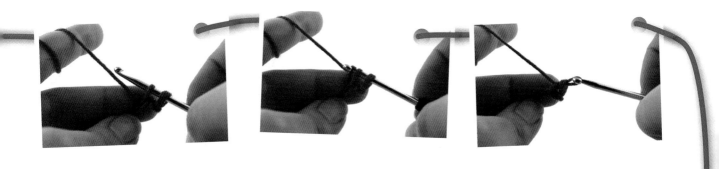

The original loop stays on your crochet hook as you do this. Now you have two loops on the crochet hook.

4 Yarn over again and pull the yarn through the two loops. Now you have one new loop, and the single crochet is done.

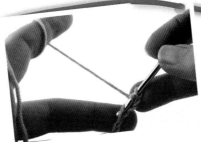

Half Double Crochet

1 Start with a slip knot and crochet a row of chain stitches. At the end, crochet 2 turning chains but do not turn the work yet.

2 Yarn over once, moving the crochet hook down, back, and then up under the working yarn to wrap the yarn around the hook.

3 Keeping the yarn over on your hook, insert the crochet hook into the third chain stitch from your hook (the stitch right before before the turning chains). There should be two strands of yarn above the hook and one strand of yarn below the hook.

4 Yarn over and pull the yarn through the stitch. Now you have a total of three loops on the crochet hook.

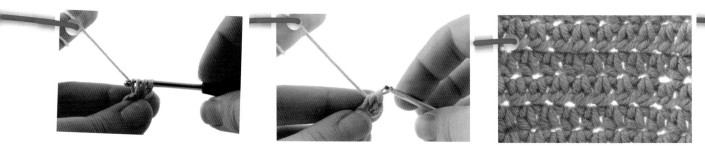

5 Yarn over again and pull the yarn through all three loops at once.

6 You now have one new loop on your hook, and the half double crochet is done. Keep going along the row, working half double crochets in each stitch in the same way. At the end of the row, crochet 2 turning chains and turn your work. Work the next row in the same way.

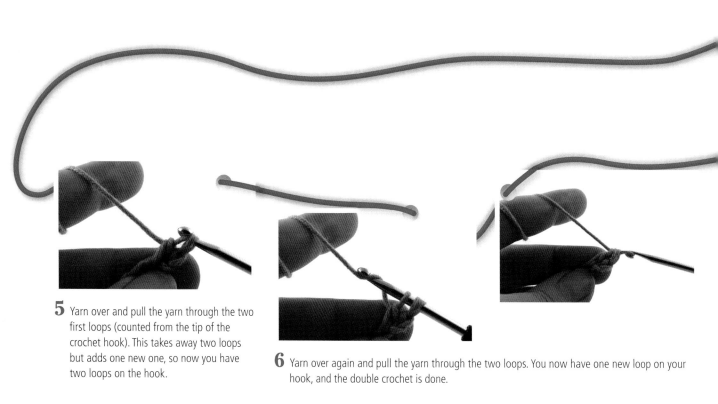

5 Yarn over and pull the yarn through the two first loops (counted from the tip of the crochet hook). This takes away two loops but adds one new one, so now you have two loops on the hook.

6 Yarn over again and pull the yarn through the two loops. You now have one new loop on your hook, and the double crochet is done.

Double Crochet

1 Start with a slip knot and crochet a row of chain stitches. At the end, crochet 3 turning chains but do not turn your work.

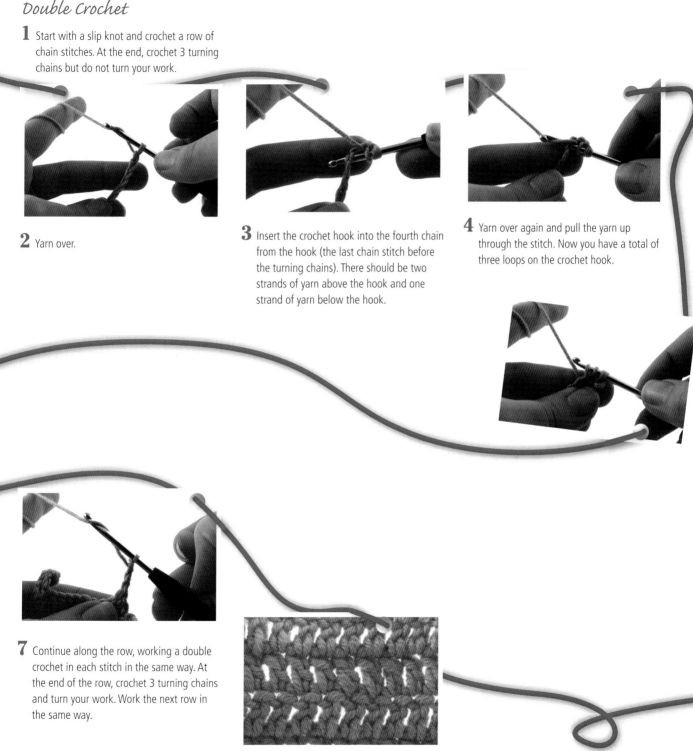

2 Yarn over.

3 Insert the crochet hook into the fourth chain from the hook (the last chain stitch before the turning chains). There should be two strands of yarn above the hook and one strand of yarn below the hook.

4 Yarn over again and pull the yarn up through the stitch. Now you have a total of three loops on the crochet hook.

7 Continue along the row, working a double crochet in each stitch in the same way. At the end of the row, crochet 3 turning chains and turn your work. Work the next row in the same way.

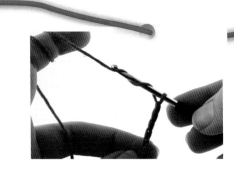

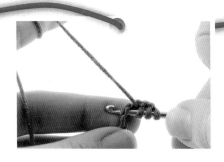

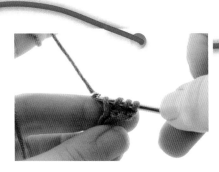

Treble Crochet

1 Start with a slip knot and crochet a row of chain stitches. At the end, crochet 4 turning chains but do not turn your work.

2 Yarn over.

3 Yarn over again so that the working yarn is wrapped around your hook two times.

4 Insert the crochet hook into the fifth chain from your hook (the last stitch before the turning chains). There should be two strands of yarn above the hook and one strand of yarn below the hook.

5 Yarn over again and pull the yarn through the stitch. Now you have a total of four loops on the crochet hook.

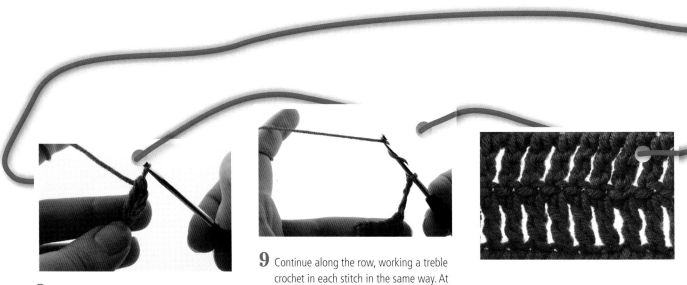

8 Yarn over one last time and pull the yarn through the last two loops. Now you have one new loop on the hook, and the treble crochet is done.

9 Continue along the row, working a treble crochet in each stitch in the same way. At the end of the row, crochet 4 turning chains and turn your work. Work the next row in the same way.

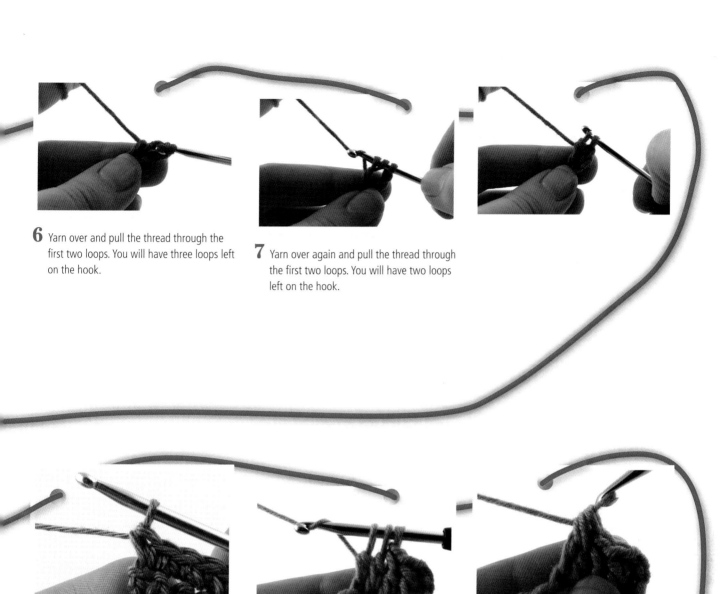

6 Yarn over and pull the thread through the first two loops. You will have three loops left on the hook.

7 Yarn over again and pull the thread through the first two loops. You will have two loops left on the hook.

Increasing

Increasing means to add stitches. To work an increase somewhere in the middle of a row, you simply work two stitches (single crochets, double crochets, or another kind—the pattern will tell you what kind of stitches to use) into a single chain stitch or a single stitch from the previous row.

If you want to increase a lot of stitches at the end of a row, like when you are crocheting a shape and want it to get much wider, crochet some extra chain stitches at the end of the row, in addition to the turning chains, to make the row longer. When you turn around to go back across the row, work stitches into the new chain stitches as well as into the stitches of the previous row.

Decreasing

When you need to reduce the number of stitches in a row, you work a decrease by working two stitches together. Work the first stitch until you are down to two loops on the hook, then go on to the next stitch. When you have three loops left in all, yarn over and pull it through all three loops on the hook.

To make a longer decrease at the end of a row, don't go all the way to the end of the row. Stop where you want the row to end, work the turning chain like you normally would, and crochet back. If you want to skip stitches at the beginning of the row, work slip stitches in the stitches you want to skip (don't work any turning chains at the beginning of this row); when you get to the place where you want to continue the regular stitches, work the number of turning chains you normally would and start crocheting across the remainder of the row.

Magic Loop

A magic loop is one way to start projects that are worked in the round (instead of back and forth in straight rows). The special thing about a magic loop is that you can pull it tight after you've put in all the stitches you need. You usually start projects that are going to be stuffed this way because it leaves a very small hole.

1 Start by wrapping the yarn around your index finger three times. The end of the yarn attached to the ball should be at the end of your finger. Hold this yarn with the thumb and middle finger of your other hand.

2 Slide the crochet hook under all the wraps of yarn, starting at the end of your finger and going toward your thumb. Catch the farthest wrap of yarn with the tip of the hook and pull it through the other two.

3 Slide the other two loops off your index finger and hold them tightly with your thumb and middle finger. The crochet hook is still in the loop you pulled through.

6 Once you have crocheted all stitches in the round, work a slip stitch in the top of the beginning chain (or chains) to connect the beginning and the end of the round.

7 Pull on the beginning thread and the hole in the middle of your magic loop will close. Pull it as tight as you can around the stitches to get a small hole.

4 Pick up the thread the way you usually would with your left hand (or right hand, for lefties), yarn over, and pull the yarn through the loop on the hook.

5 Now crochet the stitches of the first round through the hole in the middle of the ring, inserting the hook through the middle of the ring for each stitch instead of inserting it into a stitch. For a ring of single crochets, you can simply start crocheting now. For taller stitches, you'll need to start the round with the number of chains that will equal the stitch height: 2 chains for half double crochet, 3 chains for double crochet, and 4 chains for treble crochet. After the chains, crochet the stitches through the middle of the magic loop.

Starting a Round with a Ring of Chain Stitches

A round that starts with a ring of chain stitches cannot be adjusted like a magic ring. This kind of starting round is good for crocheting tube shapes and little flowers that should be open in the middle.

1 Crochet the number of chain stitches directed in the pattern and connect the last chain to the first chain stitch with a slip stitch. Make sure that the chain is not twisted when you connect it together into the ring.

2 Crochet all of the stitches of the first round into the ring that you have made. Here as well, the round has to start with a chain that matches the height of the stitches (see Magic Loop, step 5) and end with a slip stitch joining the end of the round to the beginnning.

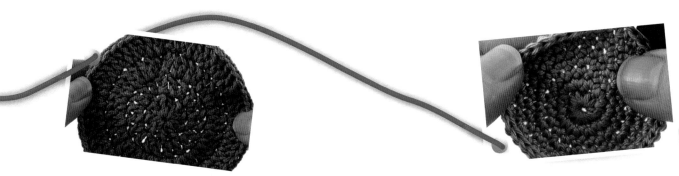

Crocheting in Even Rounds

When crocheting in even rounds, you can start with a magic loop or a ring of chain stitches. When you finish each round, join your last stitch to the first one with a slip stitch. Then start the next round with a chain that matches the height of the stitches in the round: 1 chain for single crochet, 2 chains for half double crochet, 3 chains for double crochet, and 4 chains for treble crochet.

Crocheting in a Continuous Spiral

When crocheting in spiral rounds, you can start with a magic loop or a row of chain stitches. When you finish a round, don't join the end of it—just keep working around, putting your next stitch in the first stitch of the previous round. To help you keep track of where each round started, you can slide a piece of scrap yarn in a different color through the first stitch.

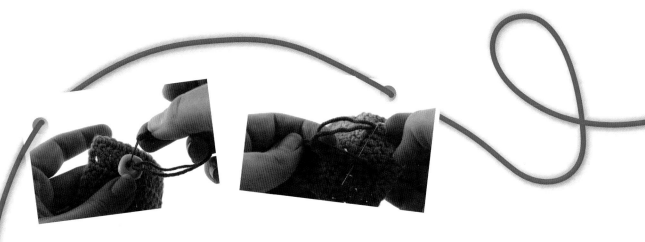

Sewing on a Button

Thread the yarn needle with a piece of yarn and knot the end of the yarn. Start at the back of the crocheted piece and stitch through the piece where you want the button to go, then through the button, from back to front. Gently pull the yarn tight, then stitch through the buttonhole and back through the crocheted fabric to the back. Repeat this step a few times and then secure the end of the yarn by sewing some stitches back and forth through just the crocheted fabric. For decorative buttons, you can just sew through the button and the fabric a few times and then tie the ends of the yarn together at the back of the work.

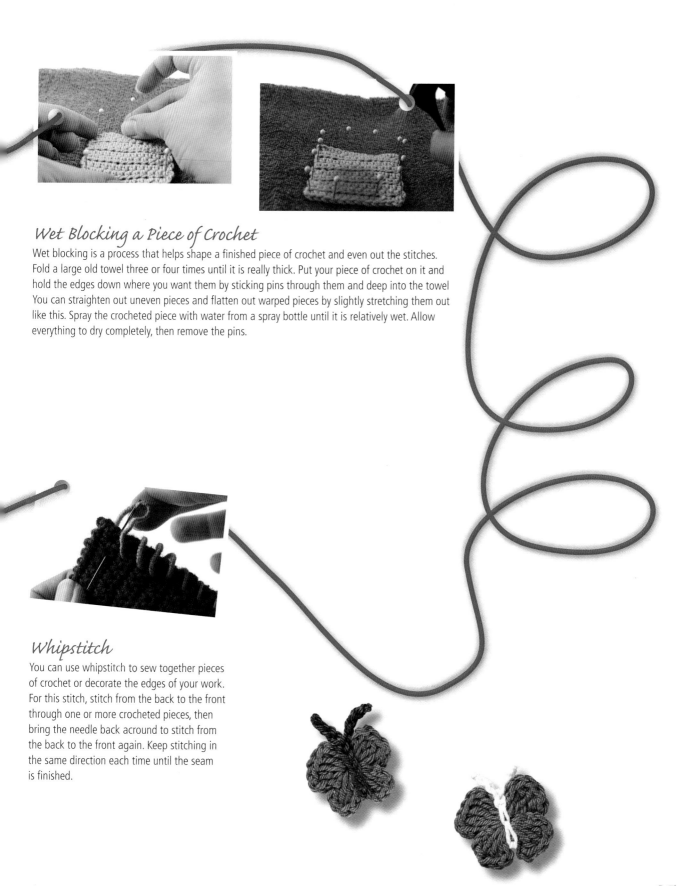

Wet Blocking a Piece of Crochet

Wet blocking is a process that helps shape a finished piece of crochet and even out the stitches. Fold a large old towel three or four times until it is really thick. Put your piece of crochet on it and hold the edges down where you want them by sticking pins through them and deep into the towel You can straighten out uneven pieces and flatten out warped pieces by slightly stretching them out like this. Spray the crocheted piece with water from a spray bottle until it is relatively wet. Allow everything to dry completely, then remove the pins.

Whipstitch

You can use whipstitch to sew together pieces of crochet or decorate the edges of your work. For this stitch, stitch from the back to the front through one or more crocheted pieces, then bring the needle back acround to stitch from the back to the front again. Keep stitching in the same direction each time until the seam is finished.

Running Stitch

Running stitch can be used to connect two flat pieces together or to add decorative stitching on the edges of a piece. Stitch from the back to the front through one or more crocehted pieces and pull the yarn tight. Then stitch in the other direction, from the front to the back, a little ways farther along the edge, and again pull the yarn tight. Keep going, alternating direction (front to back or back to front) with each stitch.

When a seam (in running stitch or whipstitch) is finished, you can secure the starting and ending threads by tying them off or by sewing through the fabric a few times in the same place with them.

Stuffing a Project

Some projects are stuffed before the crocheting is completely finished. To keep your stitches from coming unraveled while you stuff the project, pull the crochet hook out the loop and secure the loop with a safety pin. After stuffing the project, take off the safety pin and continue to crochet with the loop. Always stuff your projects with one small piece of fiberfill at a time; this makes it easier to get them into the right shape.

Sewing Parts Together

Parts of three-dimensional projects are sewn together with the whipstitch. Attach the parts beforehand with pins or some glue so they stay in the right place while you are sewing. Wherever the parts meet, stitch into one part and let the needle come out again in the other part; then go back into the first part and come out in the second part again. Repeat this around the edges where the parts meet until they are firmly connected with each other.

Using an Iron-On Patch or Fusible Web

Here is a general description on how to use iron-on products—but you should always check the manufacturer's instructions, because the process may be different for different products.

On an ironing board or old towel, spread out some parchment paper and put the piece of crochet with the front side facing down on it. Then put the iron-on patch or fusible web on it and iron over the crocheted piece for two minutes. After the piece has cooled down, cut it out from the iron-on backing. Then remove the paper backing from the crocheted piece.

Place the crocheted piece on the piece of clothing or other object you want to attach it to. Pin it firmly in place, turn the piece of clothing inside out, and iron on the inside of the fabric over where the crocheted piece is attached. After everything cools down again, you can turn your article of clothing right side out again and remove the pins.

Ready to Go!

Want to make a cool gift for your friend? How about a friendship bracelet in both of your favorite colors, a keychain, or a few hacky sacks? Or you can crochet yourself a colorful cowl or a fun hat. The detailed instructions for these projects are easy for even brand-new beginners to understand. Let's get started!

Super Easy, Super Cool

Finger Crochet Shoelaces

1 Unwind about 6 in. (15 cm) of yarn from the skein and tie a slip knot.

2 Put the thumb and index finger of your left hand through the slip knot and spread your fingers out a bit.

3 Hold the working yarn (the end connected to the skein) between the index finger and thumb of your right hand and then hold the tail of yarn from the knot steady with the rest of the fingers of the right hand.

TIP

You can also wrap gifts with these colorful ties or use them as drawstrings in jacket and sweatshirt hoods.

4 Put the middle finger of your left hand through the loop and hook it under the working yarn.

5 Use your finger to pull the yarn back through the loop.

Let the loop slip off your left thumb and index finger as you do this.

Pull on both ends until the yarn forms a chain stitch next to the starting knot.

6 Repeat steps 2 to 5 until your chain is long enough for a shoelace. You must hold onto the working yarn and the chain a little higher up each time so the yarn remains tight and the distance you have to reach to catch the yarn stays right for the size of your fingers.

7 As soon as your chain is long enough—it should be about 35 in. (90 cm) for shoelaces—cut the working yarn and pull on the last loop until the end of the yarn slips through it.

8 Cleanly cut off the beginning and end threads close to the knots and wrap each end of the chain tightly with about 1 in. (2.5 cm) of washi tape. This will make it easier to thread the shoelaces through the holes in your shoes.

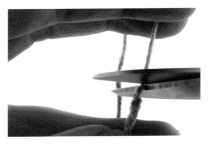

Pencil (and Crochet Hook) Jar

Decorate your Desk

You need to know how to: chain stitch

1 Tie a slip knot in the yarn.

2 Put the hook in the slip knot, pull the loop tight, then yarn over and pull the thread through the loop. You have made one chain stitch and you have a new loop on your crochet hook.

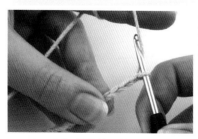

3 Crochet about 500 chain stitches like this. When you finish, carefully take your crochet hook out of it and secure the stitch with a safety pin so the chain doesn't unravel while you're doing the next few steps.

4 Stick double-sided tape around the jar, over the whole area you want to cover, then pull off the backing (if it has backing).

5 Take the starting end of your chain and press it onto the tape. You can start at either the top or bottom edge of the tape. Wrap the chain around the jar one round at a time, pressing it somewhat firmly so that it sticks and putting each round right next to the one before it. Keep going until you've covered all the tape or you reach the end of your chain. If the chain is too short to cover the tape, carefully take out the safety pin and crochet as many more chain stitches as you need. If the chain is too long, take out the safety pin and carefully pull on the working yarn to unravel one stitch at a time until the chain is the right length.

6 When the chain is the right length, cut the working yarn about 6 in. (15 cm) away from the crochet hook and thread the end through the loop. Pull firmly to tighten the knot. Cut off the extra yarn at both ends of the chain. Firmly press everything down again.

7 Now you can decorate your jar with short chains in contrasting colors. You can do a star, a bow, a spiral, stripes, or any other design. In order to get the right length of chain, you can work with a safety pin again or just keep trying the chain out as you make it until it fits. The decorations shown here each have about 45 chain stitches. Use fabric glue to attach the chains and any other decorations.

Materials

Squiggle

❀ Small amount of light (weight category 3) wool-acrylic blend yarn in light blue
❀ Small amount of light (weight category 3) wool-acrylic blend yarn in coral
❀ 1 white button, ½ in. (1 cm) wide
❀ U.S. size YY (4.0 mm) crochet hook
❀ Fabric glue
❀ Double-sided tape
❀ 12-ounce jar with a screw-on lid
❀ Scissors
❀ Safety pins

Star

❀ Small amount of light (weight category 3) wool-acrylic blend yarn in navy blue
❀ Small amount of light (weight category 3) wool-acrylic blend yarn in light blue
❀ U.S. size YY (4.0 mm) crochet hook
❀ Fabric glue
❀ Double-sided tape
❀ 12-ounce jar with a screw-on lid
❀ Scissors
❀ Safety pins

Spiral

❀ Small amount of light (weight category 3) wool-acrylic blend yarn in pink
❀ Small amount of light (weight category 3) wool-acrylic blend yarn in navy blue
❀ Small amount of light (weight category 3) wool-acrylic blend yarn in light blue
❀ U.S. size YY (4.0 mm) crochet hook
❀ Fabric glue
❀ Double-sided tape
❀ 12-ounce jar with a screw-on lid
❀ Scissors
❀ Safety pins

Bow

❀ Small amount of light (weight category 3) wool-acrylic blend yarn in pink
❀ Small amount of light (weight category 3) wool-acrylic blend yarn in light blue
❀ U.S. size YY (4.0 mm) crochet hook
❀ Fabric glue
❀ Double-sided tape
❀ 12-ounce jar with a screw-on lid
❀ Scissors
❀ Safety pins

Stripes

❀ Small amount of light (weight category 3) wool-acrylic blend yarn in navy blue
❀ Small amount of light (weight category 3) wool-acrylic blend yarn in coral
❀ 3 pink buttons, ½ in. (1 cm) wide
❀ U.S. size YY (4.0 mm) crochet hook
❀ Fabric glue
❀ Double-sided tape
❀ 12-ounce jar with a screw-on lid
❀ Scissors
❀ Safety pins

Materials

Crocodile

- ❀ Small amount fine (weight category 2) cotton yarn in pink
- ❀ 1 crocodile button, 1 in. (2 cm) long
- ❀ U.S. size yy (2.5 mm) crochet hook
- ❀ 1 button, ½ in. (1 cm) wide
- ❀ Scissors
- ❀ Yarn needle
- ❀ Sewing needle and thread if the holes in the buttons are too small for a yarn needle

Stars

- ❀ Small amount fine (weight category 2) cotton yarn in navy blue
- ❀ 5 star-shaped buttons, ½ in. (1 cm) wide
- ❀ U.S. size yy (2.5 mm) crochet hook
- ❀ 1 button, ½ in. (1 cm) wide
- ❀ Scissors

- ❀ Yarn needle
- ❀ A little bit of extra yarn in a different color for sewing on the buttons
- ❀ Sewing needle and thread if the holes in the buttons are too small for a yarn needle

Beads

- ❀ Small amount fine (weight category 2) cotton yarn in coral
- ❀ 9 white glass beads, ¼ in. (0.8 cm) wide
- ❀ U.S. size yy (2.5 mm) crochet hook
- ❀ 1 button, ½ in. (1 cm) wide
- ❀ Scissors
- ❀ Yarn needle
- ❀ Sewing needle and thread if the holes in the button or beads are too small for a yarn needle

Suns

- ❀ Small amount fine (weight category 2) cotton yarn in red

- ❀ 4 pink sun buttons, ¾ in. (1.5 cm) wide
- ❀ U.S. size yy (2.5 mm) crochet hook
- ❀ 1 button, ½ in. (1 cm) wide
- ❀ Scissors
- ❀ Yarn needle
- ❀ Sewing needle and thread if the holes in the buttons are too small for a yarn needle

Striped Buttons

- ❀ Small amount fine (weight category 2) cotton yarn in mint green
- ❀ 5 pink-and-white striped buttons, ½ in. (1 cm) wide
- ❀ U.S. size yy (2.5 mm) crochet hook
- ❀ 1 button, ½ in. (1 cm) wide
- ❀ Scissors
- ❀ Yarn needle
- ❀ A little bit of extra yarn in a different color for sewing on the buttons
- ❀ Sewing needle and thread if the holes in the buttons are too small for a yarn needle

For Best Friends

Cool Friendship Bracelets

You need to know how to: chain stitch, single crochet, slip stitch, sew on buttons

1 Tie a slip knot. Crochet 35 chain stitches, then a 36th chain stitch for the turning chain. Don't turn the work yet.

2 **Row 1:** Insert the hook into the second chain from the hook, yarn over, and pull up a loop (two loops on the hook). Yarn over again and pull through both loops. You have completed your first single crochet stitch. Work 1 single crochet in each chain stitch until you get to the end of the chain.

3 **Row 2:** Turn the piece upside down so the foundation chain is on top and Row 1 is on the bottom. Insert the hook into the bottom loop (now on the top edge) of the closest

chain to the end, yarn over, and pull up a loop (two loops on the hook). Yarn over again and pull the yarn through both loops. You have completed a single crochet stitch. Do the same with the rest of the chains along the edge. When you get to the end, chain 6.

4 **Row 3:** Insert the hook into the top of the first single crochet of Row 1. Yarn over, then pull the yarn through the stitch and the loop on your hook to work a slip stitch closing up the chain loop.

5 Cut the working yarn about 4 in. (10 cm) from the loop. Put the end of the yarn

through the loop and pull to tighten the loop around the end. Use a yarn needle to weave the tail of the yarn into the crocheted fabric for about 1 in. (2.5 cm), then trim the rest of the tail. Hide the tail at the beginning in the same way.

6 Sew the button onto the end of the bracelet opposite from the chain loop. Now you can fasten your friendship bracelet around your wrist.

7 Finish by decorating your friendship bracelet by sewing beads or more buttons onto it.

TIP

A fun bracelet like this is even more special when it was made with a specific friend in mind. Try out the designs shown here, but also come up with your own versions in your friends' favorite colors or decorated with things they love.

Crochet Calligraphy

Another Creative Use for Chains

Materials

Hearts

- Small amount of light (weight category 3) wool-acrylic blend yarn in light pink
- Small amount of light (weight category 3) wool-acrylic blend yarn in medium pink
- Small amount of light (weight category 3) wool-acrylic blend yarn in medium blue
- U.S. size yy (4.0 mm) crochet hook
- 3 light yellow buttons, ½ in. (1 cm) wide
- Brown cardstock or sturdy construction paper
- Scissors
- Hole punch
- Pencil
- Tape
- Craft glue

Circle

- Small amount of light (weight category 3) wool-acrylic blend yarn in light pink
- Small amount of light (weight category 3) wool-acrylic blend yarn in aqua
- U.S. size yy (4.0 mm) crochet hook
- 5 medium blue beads, ⅛ in. (4 mm) wide
- 9 light blue beads, ⅛ in. (4 mm) wide
- 3 white beads, ⅛ in. (4 mm) wide
- Pink acrylic paint
- Cardboard
- Pencil
- Compass (or a round plate or bowl to trace)
- Scissors
- Paintbrush
- Glue

You need to know how to: chain stitch

Hearts

1 Draw the hearts on the construction paper and cut them out. The little hearts we used are about 4 in. (10 cm) tall and the large hearts about 8 in. (21 cm) tall. Punch a hole on both sides of the big heart near the top

2 Crochet a chain to go around the edge of each heart, using the light and medium pink yarns. Look at steps 2 to 6 on the next page if you need a reminder of how to do chain stitch. Our little hearts needed chains of 50 stitches each, and the large heart needed a chain 130 stitches long. Test your chains every now and then to see how much more you need. Fasten off the chains when they are long enough by cutting the yarn and pulling on the last loop until the end pulls through

3 Crochet other chains with light pink for the letters and medium pink for the flowers. The flowers consist of about 32 chains each; the number of chains needed for the letters will depend on what letters you are using. Fasten off the chains when they are long enough.

4 Crochet a chain from medium blue to hang the project. When it is long enough, fasten it off.

5 Glue all the chains and buttons onto the hearts. Thread the blue chain through the holes at the top of the big heart and tie the ends together. To connect the little hearts with the big one, cut a long piece of blue yarn and tape it to the back of the three hearts.

Circle

1 Using a compass, draw a circle with a diameter of about 8 in. (20 cm) on the cardboard. You can also trace around a plate or a bowl. Cut out the circle, paint it with acrylic paint, and let it dry.

2 Tie a slip knot with the pink yarn.

3 Put the slip knot on the hook and pull the yarn to tighten the loop around the hook. Yarn over and pull the yarn through the loop. This gives you 1 chain stitch and a new loop on your hook.

4 Crochet about 100 chain stitches like this.

5 When you have about 100 chains, carefully pull your crochet hook out of the loop and secure the stitch with a safety pin.

6 Place your chain row of chain stitches around the edge of the circle to test its size. If the chain is not long enough, remove the safety pin, put the hook back in the loop, and crochet more chains. If the chain is too long, remove the safety pin and carefully pull out some of the stitches.

7 When the chain is the right length, cut the yarn about 6 in. (15 cm) from the hook and thread the end through the loop. Pull firmly to tighten the knot.

8 For the inner edging, crochet another chain in the same way, using the aqua yarn.

9 Next, make the extra decorative chains. The short chain at the bottom of the circle is about 20 stitches and the squiggle at the top is about 40 chains.

10 Now, make the chain for the letters. The chain for the name Lena is about 200 chains long, but depending on how long your name is, you may need more or fewer chains. For really long names, you might need a bigger circle. When the chain is long enough, fasten it off.

11 Glue all the chains and beads to the cardboard.

Keychain Wristbands

Quick and Practical

You need to know how to: chain stitch, single crochet, slip stitch, and embroider or sew

Materials

- ❀ 1 skein (1.8 oz/50 g) of fine (weight category 2) cotton yarn in aqua
- ❀ Small amount of fine (weight category 2) cotton yarn in white
- ❀ Small amount of fine (weight category 2) cotton yarn in pink
- ❀ 1 key ring, 1 in. (2.5 cm) wide
- ❀ 1 metal crimp end for ribbons or bracelets that can attach to the key ring
- ❀ U.S. size YY (3.0 mm) crochet hook
- ❀ Scissors
- ❀ Yarn needle
- ❀ Flat-nosed pliers

1 Start with a slip knot with aqua yarn. Chain 6, then make 1 more chain for the turning chain (don't turn the piece now).

2 Work 1 single crochet in the second chain from your hook and in each of the remaining chains—6 single crochets in all. Turn your work.

3 Chain 1 (turning chain), then single crochet in each stitch across—6 single crochets. Turn your work.

4 Crochet 56 rows as described in Step 3.

5 Cut the yarn about 6 in. (15 cm) from the crochet hook and thread the end through the loop. Pull firmly to tighten the knot.

6 Use a yarn needle to weave the yarn tails at the beginning and end of the piece into the fabric for about 1 in. (2.5 cm), then trim them. Thread the yarn needle with about 20 in. (50 cm) of pink yarn and sew decorative crosswise stitches along the band. Fasten off the end of the yarn.

7 Attach the white yarn anywhere on the edge of the band by putting a slip knot on the crochet hook then working a slip stitch through the end of any row. Work a single crochet in the same row end, then chain 1. Skip one row end and work a single crochet in the next row end, then chain 1. Continue around the band, alternating between 1 single crochet and 1 chain stitch and skipping every other row end so that the stitches are evenly spaced along the edge and not crowded. Work around all four sides of the piece in this way.

8 When you get back to where you started, work a slip stitch in the top of the first single crochet to join the last stitch to the first one. Cut the working yarn about 6 in. (15 cm) from the hook and thread the end through the loop. Pull firmly to tighten the knot. Use a yarn needle to weave this tail into the white stitches to hide it.

9 Fold your band in half, with the right side (the nice-looking side) on the outside. Slide both ends into the crimp end and firmly squeeze it together. You can use flat-nose pliers to do this or ask an adult to help you.

10 Attach your key ring to the crimp end, and you're finished!

Little Monsters

The Invasion Begins Now

You need to know how to: make a magic loop, chain stitch, single crochet, slip stitch, and double crochet

Materials

Aqua Monster

- 1 skein (1.8 oz./50 g) of fine (weight category 2) cotton yarn in aqua
- Small amount of fine (weight category 2) cotton yarn in red
- Small amount of fine (weight category 2) cotton yarn in navy blue
- Small amount of fine (weight category 2) cotton yarn in white
- 2 pink beads, ¼ in. (0.8 cm) wide
- U.S. size YY (3.0 mm) crochet hook
- Scissors
- Yarn needle
- Fabric glue
- Permanent felt-tip marker

Navy Blue Monster

- 1 skein (1.8 oz./50 g) of fine (weight category 2) cotton yarn in navy blue
- Small amount of fine (weight category 2) cotton yarn in aqua
- Small amount of fine (weight category 2) cotton yarn in lime green
- Small amount of fine (weight category 2) cotton yarn in white
- 1 purple bead, ¼ in. (0.8 cm) wide
- U.S. size YY (3.0 mm) crochet hook
- Scissors
- Yarn needle
- Fabric glue
- Permanent felt-tip marker

(See page 45 for the materials needed for the other monsters)

1 With your main color, make a magic loop.

2 Round 1: Work 10 single crochets in the magic loop. Pull on the end of the yarn until the magic loop closes and you get a little flat circle.

3 Round 2: Work 2 single crochets into every stitch of the previous round. In this project, you will work in a spiral (see page 24). Use the crochet hook to pull a scrap of yarn in a different color through the first stitch of the round to mark where the round starts.

4 Round 3: Work 1 single crochet into every stitch of the previous round.

5 Round 4: Work 1 single crochet in the first stitch, then work 2 single crochets in the second stitch. Repeat around in this pattern, increasing in every other stitch.

6 Round 5: Same as Round 3.

7 Round 6: Work 1 single crochet in each of the first two stitches, then work 2 single crochets in the third stitch. Repeat around in this pattern, increasing in every third stitch.

8 **Rounds 7 to 19:** Same as Round 3. Fasten off the work at the end of Round 19 by cutting the yarn about 6 in. (15 cm) from the hook, pulling the end through the loop, and pulling tight.

9 **Round 20:** With the edging color, make a slip knot and put the knot on your crochet hook. Join the yarn anywhere on the edge of the monster by working a slip stitch in any stitch along the edge. Chain 1, then single crochet in the same stitch you worked the slip stitch in and in every other stitch around.

10 When you get back to where you started, work a slip stitch in the beginning chain to join the end of the round to the beginning. Cut the yarn about 6 in. (15 cm) from the hook and thread the end through the loop. Pull to tighten the knot. Cut the main color as well and use a yarn needle to weave both yarn ends into the stitches of the same color to hide them.

11 Cut a piece of thread in the main color about 8 in. (20 cm) and insert it into the monster wherever you want an antenna to be. Pull both ends of the yarn to the outside and even them out so they are both the same length, then tie them together about ten times. Thread a bead onto one of the strands, then knot them two more times. Add as many antennae as you like to your monster.

12 To make the eyes, start with a magic loop in white and work 10 double crochet stitches into it. Pull on the yarn to close your magic loop. Work a slip stitch in the first double crochet to join the beginning and end of the round.

13 Cut the yarn about 6 in. (15 cm) away from the hook and thread the end through the loop. Pull to tighten the knot. Weave the end of the yarn into the stitches with a yarn needle.

TIP

Crochet a personalized monster in the favorite colors of each member of your family.

14 Make another eye. Attach both eyes to the monster with fabric glue. Draw the pupils with a permanent marker.

15 Make a chain 12 stitches long for the mouth and fasten it off by cutting the yarn and pulling the end through the loop. Cut the beginning and ending threads short and glue the mouth onto the monster.

Materials

Red Monster

* 1 skein (1.8 oz./50 g) of fine (weight category 2) cotton yarn in red
* Small amount of fine (weight category 2) cotton yarn in lime green
* Small amount of fine (weight category 2) cotton yarn in aqua
* Small amount of fine (weight category 2) cotton yarn in white
* 2 white beads, ¼ in. (0.8 cm) wide
* U.S. size YY (3.0 mm) crochet hook
* Scissors
* Yarn needle
* Fabric glue
* Permanent felt-tip marker

Green Monster

* 1 skein (1.8 oz./50 g) of fine (weight category 2) cotton yarn in lime green
* Small amount of fine (weight category 2) cotton yarn in navy blue
* Small amount of fine (weight category 2) cotton yarn in red
* Small amount of fine (weight category 2) cotton yarn in white
* 2 blue beads, ¼ in. (0.8 cm) wide
* U.S. size YY (3.0 mm) crochet hook
* Scissors
* Yarn needle
* Fabric glue
* Permanent felt-tip marker

Colorful Cowl

Cute and Easy to Make

You need to know how to: chain stitch, double crochet, slip stitch, and sew on buttons

1 Crochet 100 chain stitches with the gray-blue yarn (color A). Attach the pink yarn (color F). Cut the blue yarn, leaving about 6 in. (15 cm) as a tail.

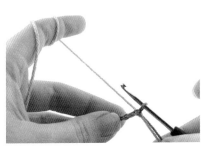

2 Work 3 turning chains, then crochet back along the row in double crochet with the pink yarn (100 double crochets in all). Attach the aqua yarn (color G) and cut off the pink yarn, leaving a 6 in. (15 cm) tail. Turn your work.

3 Work 3 turning chains, then work another row of 100 double crochets. Attach the next color (see step 4), cut off the old color, and turn your work.

4 Repeat step 3 sixteen times in all, following this color pattern: C, E, B, H, G, D, E, F, C, H, G, B, E, D, C, F.

5 Use a yarn needle to weave all the tails into the stitches of the same color to hide them; trim the ends.

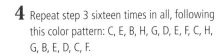

Materials

❀ 1 skein (1.8 oz./50 g) light (weight category 3) acrylic-wool blend yarn in gray-blue (color A)

❀ 1 skein (1.8 oz./50 g) light (weight category 3) acrylic-wool blend yarn in cream (color B)

❀ 1 skein (1.8 oz./50 g) light (weight category 3) acrylic-wool blend yarn in light yellow (color C)

❀ 1 skein (1.8 oz./50 g) light (weight category 3) acrylic-wool blend yarn in light blue (color D)

❀ 1 skein (1.8 oz./50 g) light (weight category 3) acrylic-wool blend yarn in red (color E)

❀ 1 skein (1.8 oz./50 g) light (weight category 3) acrylic-wool blend yarn in pink (color F)

❀ 1 skein (1.8 oz./50 g) light (weight category 3) acrylic-wool blend yarn in aqua (color G)

❀ 1 skein (1.8 oz./50 g) light (weight category 3) acrylic-wool blend yarn in purple (color H)

❀ 2 red round buttons, ½ in. (1.5 cm) wide

❀ 2 yellow star buttons, ½ in. (1.5 cm) wide

❀ 2 round turquoise buttons, ½ in. (1.5 cm) wide

❀ 2 round orange buttons with flowers, ½ in. (1.5 cm) wide

❀ U.S. size yy (3.5 mm) crochet hook

❀ Yarn needle

❀ Sewing needle and sewing thread in a few colors if the holes in the buttons are too small for a yarn needle

6 Now crochet around the edge of the whole piece. Attach the gray-blue yarn at one corner by putting a slip knot on the hook and then working a slip stitch where you want to attach the yarn. Chain 3 (this counts as the first couble crochet), then crochet along the long edge of the piece, putting 1 double crochet in each stitch. At the corner, put 3 double crochets in the corner so the edging goes around the corner evenly. Now crochet along the short side, putting 2 or 3 double crochets (however many will fit in nicely, without the stitches being too crowded or too stretched out) in the sideways double crochet at the end of each row. Go around the other long and short sides and corners in the same way.

7 When you get to the last corner, work a slip stitch in the top chain of the beginning 3 chains, then work 3 more chains and turn your work so the short edge is on top and the hook and working yarn are at the right side of the piece (for right-handers; for lefties they should be on the left side).

8 Work 1 double crochet in each stitch across the short edge. When you get to the corner, stop, work 3 turning chains, and turn your work.

9 Make six more rows as described in step 8. Then cut the yarn about 6 in. (15 cm) from the hook and thread the end through the loop. Pull to tighten the knot, then use a yarn needle to weave the end into the fabric.

10 Now fold the scarf as shown in the picture: Place the short edges on top of each other and fold the blue-gray part you just made back on itself so that you have three layers on top of each other.

11 Hold the three layers in place with a few pins and sew the buttons on along the band with a yarn needle and leftover pieces of yarn (or with a sewing needle and sewing thread in various colors if the yarn needle won't fit through the holes in the buttons). As you sew on the buttons, make sure that you go through all three layers every time.

12 Secure the yarn for the buttons on the inside by knotting the starting and ending tails together. Trim the ends of the yarn short.

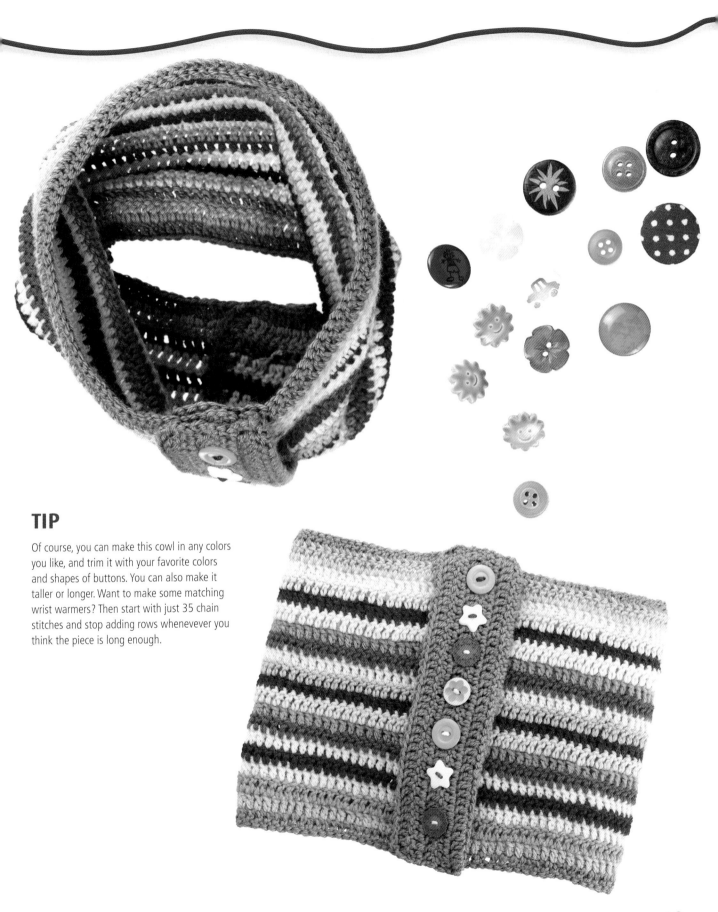

TIP

Of course, you can make this cowl in any colors you like, and trim it with your favorite colors and shapes of buttons. You can also make it taller or longer. Want to make some matching wrist warmers? Then start with just 35 chain stitches and stop adding rows whenever you think the piece is long enough.

49

For Odds and Ends
A Crocheted Basket for Your Hooks and Yarn

You need to know how to: chain stitch, single crochet, decrease, and sew on buttons

1 Start with a slip knot in blue yarn, then chain 26 (25 foundation chains plus 1 turning chain).

2 Single crochet in the second chain from your hook and in every chain across—25 single crochets. Turn your work.

3 Chain 1. Work 1 single crochet in each stitch across. Turn.

4 Work 24 more rows the same way as in step 3. This will give you a square. Everybody crochets a little differently. If you don't have a square at this point, add a few more rows or carefully pull out a few rows until you do. Or you can just keep going with a rectangle to make a rectangular basket.

5 Now crochet all the way around the edge of the square as follows: chain 1, skip 1 stitch and single crochet in the next stitch; repeat this pattern, alternating 1 chain (and skipping the stitch underneath) and 1 single crochet. On the sides of the piece, put your single crochets in the turning chains at the end of every other row and the chains/skips in between them.

6 When you get back to where you started, work another round all the way around, working 1 single crochet in each single crochet or chain of the previous round. Single crochet 2 together at each corner.

7 Work 16 more rounds of single crochet around the piece, working 1 stitch in each stitch of the previous round. When you finish the last round, join the pink yarn and cut off the blue yarn.

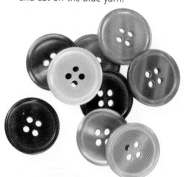

8 Now work 9 more rounds of single crochet with pink. At the end, work a slip stitch in the first stitch of the next round to even out the end of the round, then cut the yarn and pull the end through the loop, pulling the knot tight. Use the yarn needle to weave in all the tails.

Materials

- 2 skeins (1.8 oz./50 g each) light (weight category 3) cotton-acrylic blend yarn in blue
- 1 skein (1.8 oz./50 g) light (weight category 3) cotton-acrylic blend yarn in pink
- Assorted buttons, about 1 in. (2.5 cm) wide
- U.S. size yy (4.5 mm) crochet hook
- Scissors
- Yarn needle
- Glue (optional)

9 Fold over the pink part of the basket to the outside. Sew the buttons around the edge.

10 You can also glue the buttons on if you prefer.

TIP

Want your basket to be a bit stiffer? You can get fabric stiffeners that will make your basket a little sturdier at craft stores. Some are spray-on and some you soak your project in, so read the directions carefully to know how to use the product. Use the fabric stiffener and let it dry completely, then attach the buttons.

Brimmed Cap

A Cool Hat for Boys and Girls

You need to know how to: make a magic loop, chain stitch, slip stitch, single crochet, and increase

1 Start with a magic loop.

2 **Round 1:** Work 10 single crochets in the magic loop.

3 **Round 2:** Continuing around in a spiral, work 2 single crochets in every stitch of the previous round (20 single crochets in all).

4 Use a short scrap of yarn in a different color to mark the beginning of the round to help you keep track of where you are.

5 **Round 3:** Work 1 single crochet in the next stitch, then work 2 single crochets in the next stitch. Continue around in this pattern, increasing in every other stitch.

6 **Round 4:** Work 1 single crochet in every stitch of the previous round.

7 **Round 5:** Work 1 single crochet in each of the next 2 stitches, then work 2 single crochets in the next stitch. Continue around in this pattern, increasing in every third stitch.

8 **Round 6:** Same as Round 4.

9 **Round 7:** Work 1 single crochet in each of the next 3 stitches, then work 2 single crochets in the next stitch. Continue around in this pattern, increasing in every fourth stitch.

Materials

Pink Hat

- ❀ 1 skein (3.5 oz/100 g) bulky (weight category 5) acrylic-wool blend yarn in pink
- ❀ U.S. size yy (8.0 mm) crochet hook
- ❀ Scissors
- ❀ Yarn needle

Green Hat

- ❀ 1 skein (3.5 oz/100 g) bulky (weight category 5) acrylic-wool blend yarn in green
- ❀ U.S. size yy (8.0 mm) crochet hook
- ❀ Scissors
- ❀ Yarn needle

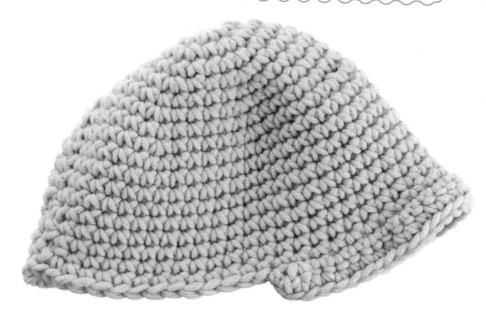

10 **Rounds 8–20:** Same as Round 4.

11 **Row 21 (start brim):** Mark the beginning of this row. Single crochet in the next 20 stitches, then work 1 slip stitch in the next stitch. Turn your work.

12 **Row 22:** Chain 1. Single crochet in the first stitch of the previous row, then work 2 single crochets in the next stitch; continue in this pattern, increasing in every other stitch, until you get to the beginning of the row.

13 Slip stitch in the next stitch, then turn your work.

14 **Row 23:** Chain 1. Single crochet in each stitch across the brim. When you get to the end, single crochet in the next stitch of Round 20, then slip stitch in the next stitch. Fasten off by cutting the yarn and pulling the end through the loop. Weave in all the yarn ends with the yarn needle.

TIP

Decorate your cap with buttons or pins. You can also sew on a pom-pom or chains in different colors.

Tricks and Kicks

Hacky Sacks to Make Yourself

You need to know how to: make a magic loop, single crochet, increase, and decrease

1 Start with a magic loop in the main color.

2 **Round 1:** Work 6 single crochets in the magic loop. Pull on the starting yarn to close the loop. Join the end of the round to the beginning by working 1 slip stitch in the first stitch.

3 **Round 2:** Work 2 single crochets in every stitch of the previous round. Use a short scrap of yarn in a different color to mark the beginning of the round.

4 **Round 3:** Work 1 single crochet in the next stitch, then work 2 single crochets in the next stitch. Continue around in this pattern, increasing in every other stitch.

5 **Round 4:** Work 1 single crochet in each of the next 2 stitches, then work 2 single crochets in the next stitch. Continue around in this pattern, increasing in every third stitch.

6 **Round 5:** Work 1 single crochet in each of the next 3 stitches, then work 2 single crochets in the next stitch. Continue around in this pattern, increasing in every fourth stitch.

7 **Round 6:** Work 1 single crochet in each of the next 4 stitches, then work 2 single crochets in the next stitch. Continue around in this pattern, increasing in every fifth stitch.

8 **Round 7:** Work 1 single crochet in each of the next 5 stitches, then work 2 single crochets in the next stitch. Continue around in this pattern, increasing in every sixth stitch.

9 **Round 8–18:** Work 1 single crochet in every stitch of the previous round. At the beginning of Round 10, change to the stripe color. Don't cut the main color, but keep it on the inside of the piece. When you get to the end of the round, pick up the main color again and crochet Round 11 with it; don't cut off the stripe color. Work Rounds 12, 13, and 15 in the stripe color and Round 14 in the main color. At the end of Round 15, cut off the stripe color and continue in the main color.

10 **Round 19:** Single crochet in the first 5 stitches, then single crochet 2 together in the next 2 stitches. Continue around in this pattern, decreasing after every 5 stitches.

11 **Round 20:** Single crochet in the first 4 stitches, then single crochet 2 together in the next 2 stitches. Continue around in this pattern.

TIP

Crochet very tightly as you make the hacky sack so you don't leave any gaps for the filling to fall through. If your crocheting is too loose, you can try using a smaller hook to help make it tighter.

Materials

Navy Blue Hacky Sack

❀ 1 skein (1.8 oz./50 g) fine (weight category 2) cotton yarn in navy blue

❀ Small amount of fine (weight category 2) cotton yarn in lime green

❀ About ½ cup of dried beans, rice, or plastic pellets

❀ U.S. size YY (2.5 mm) crochet hook

❀ Scissors

❀ Yarn needle

Red Hacky Sack

❀ 1 skein (1.8 oz./50 g) fine (weight category 2) cotton yarn in red

❀ Small amount of fine (weight category 2) cotton yarn in aqua

❀ About ½ cup of dried beans, rice, or plastic pellets

❀ U.S. size YY (2.5 mm) crochet hook

❀ Scissors

❀ Yarn needle

Aqua Hacky Sack

❀ 1 skein (1.8 oz./50 g) fine (weight category 2) cotton yarn in aqua

❀ Small amount of fine (weight category 2) cotton yarn in navy blue

❀ About ½ cup of dried beans, rice, or plastic pellets

❀ U.S. size YY (2.5 mm) crochet hook

❀ Scissors

❀ Yarn needle

57

12 **Round 21:** Single crochet in the first 3 stitches, then single crochet 2 together in the next 2 stitches. Continue around in this pattern.

13 **Round 22:** Single crochet in the first 2 stitches, then single crochet 2 together in the next 2 stitches. Continue around in this pattern.

14 **Round 23:** Single crochet in the first stitch, then single crochet 2 together in the next 2 stitches. Continue around in this pattern.

15 **Round 24:** Single crochet 2 together in each pair of stitches around.

16 Cut the yarn about 8 in. (20 cm) from the crochet hook. Thread the end through the loop and pull the knot tight.

17 You can now fill your hacky sack with rice, dried beans, or plastic pellets. If you want to be able to wash the hacky sack, plastic pellets are best.

18 Us your crochet hook or a yarn needle to thread the long tail at the end of the project through all the stitches of the last round. Pull this tail tight to close up the top of the hacky sack. Tie the yarn off, trim it, and weave the end into the fabric to hide it.

TIP

Depending on the filling type and amount you use, the hacky sacks will have different weights. If you make three of these hacky sacks, you can use them as juggling bags.

TIP

Hacky sacks filled with beans or rice are also great hand warmers in the winter! Place them in the microwave for one minute on medium-low power and then put them in the pockets of your coat to keep your hands warm while you wait for the school bus.

Snail Hair Ties

Spirals to Wear in Your Hair

You need to know how to: chain stitch, slip stitch, single crochet, increase, whipstitch, and embroider

1 With the main color, chain 4. Join into a ring by working a slip stitch in the first chain.

2 Round 1: Work 2 single crochets in each stitch of the ring.

3 Round 2: Use a scrap of yarn in a different color to mark the beginning of the round. Continuing to crochet around in a spiral, single crochet in the next stitch, then work 2 single crochet in the next stitch. Continue in this pattern around the circle, increasing in every other stitch.

4 Round 3: Single crochet in the next 2 stitches, then work 2 single crochet in the next stitch. Continue in this pattern around the circle.

5 Round 5: Single crochet in the next 3 stitches, then work 2 single crochet in the next stitch. Continue in this pattern around the circle.

6 Round 5: Single crochet in the next 4 stitches, then work 2 single crochet in the next stitch. Continue in this pattern around the circle.

7 Work a slip stitch in the next stitch to even out the end of the round, then cut the yarn about 8 in. (20 cm) from the hook and thread the end through the loop. Pull on the yarn to tighten the knot.

8 Thread the yarn tail into a yarn needle and go around the edge of the circle in whipstitch, putting one stitch into each single crochet around the edge.

9 Place the button on your crocheted circle, hold it firmly, and carefully pull on the yarn. The edges will pull together and around the button. You may have to hold the button tightly to keep it from slipping. The tighter you pull, the fewer stitches will be on top of the button. You will embroider the top of the button later.

10 When the button cover is as tight as you want it to be, tie off the yarn, trim it, and weave the end into the fabric.

11 Thread the yarn needle with a different color of yarn and pick a starting point anywhere along the edge. Embroider a spiral on the button, going into the gaps between the crochet stitches.

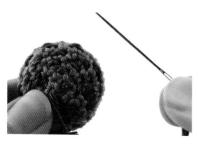

12 Secure the thread at the end by taking a couple of stitches in the same place, then weave the end into the inside of the button and trim.

13 Cut the hair elastic close to the joint. (If it's the kind with a metal joint, cut that part off completely and throw it away.) Turn the button over and thread the elastic through the hole in the button shank. Tie the ends of the elastic together, then pull it so that the knot is right next to the shank.

Materials

Two-Tone Teal Hair Tie

- ❀ Small amount of fine (weight category 2) cotton yarn in aqua (main color)
- ❀ Small amount of fine (weight category 2) cotton yarn in teal
- ❀ Purple shank button, 1 in. (2.5 cm) wide
- ❀ Blue hair elastic thin enough to go through the hole in the button shank, about 4 in. (10 cm) around
- ❀ U.S. size YY (3.0 mm) crochet hook
- ❀ Scissors
- ❀ Yarn needle

TIP

You can also string two or more buttons on the same hair elastic. Or you can use the buttons like normal buttons on bags and jackets.

Cute Leg Warmers

Keep Your Legs Warm All Year Round

You need to know how to: chain stitch and double crochet

Materials

Blue Leg Warmers

- 1 skein (3.5 oz./100 g) bulky (weight category 5) acrylic yarn in blue
- 35 in. (90 cm) pink satin ribbon, 2 cm wide
- U.S. size yy (5.0 mm) crochet hook
- Scissors
- Safety Pin
- Yarn needle

Purple Leg Warmers

- 1 skein (3.5 oz./100 g) bulky (weight category 5) acrylic yarn in purple
- 35 in. (90 cm) blue satin ribbon, 2 cm wide
- U.S. size yy (5.0 mm) crochet hook
- Scissors
- Safety Pin
- Yarn needle

1 Start with a slip knot and crochet 35 chain stitches.

2 Make the chain into a ring, making sure you don't twist the strand. Join the last chain to the first chain with a slip stitch.

3 **Round 1:** Chain 3, then work 1 double crochet in the first chain.

4 Double crochet in every chain around the ring.

5 Join the last double crochet to the beginning of the round by working a slip stitch in the top chain of the beginning 3 chains.

6 **Round 2:** Chain 3, then double crochet in each stitch around. Join the last double crochet to the beginning of the round by working a slip stitch in the top chain of the beginning 3 chains.

7 **Rounds 3–19:** Same as Round 2.

8 Cut the yarn about 6 in. (15 cm) from the hook and thread the end through the loop. Pull on the yarn to tighten the knot. Use a yarn needle to weave the beginning and ending tails of yarn into the crocheted fabric.

10 Cut the ribbon in half and pin the safety pin to the end of one of the halves to help you thread it through the fabric. Take one of the leg warmers and find the second row of double crochet from the top edge. Starting in the middle of the front (the part where you can see the joins between the rows should go in the back), thread the safety pin between two stitches, behind two double crochets, then back out in the next gap between stitches. Skip two double crochets and weave it back through the next gap. Continue to weave the ribbon between stitches until you get back to where you started. Both ends of the ribbon should end up on the outside of the leg warmer, but if something goes wrong, you can just skip a few stitches so that they both come out in front. Thread the other half of the ribbon into the second leg warmer in the same way.

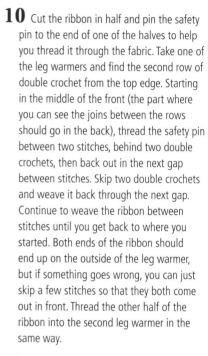

9 Repeat steps 1 to 8 to make a second leg warmer.

11 Try the leg warmers on and tighten the ribbon so they fit your leg. Tie the ribbon in a bow.

12 Cut off the ends of the ribbon at an angle. If the ends of the ribbon start to unravel, you can put some glue on them so they stay neat and smooth.

TIP

You can also braid or crochet ties for your leg warmers out of yarn. If you like, you can decorate the ends of the ties with pom-poms.

Moving Up

Closet full of boring old jeans and T-shirts? No problem! With cool stars and other crocheted motifs, you can make your clothes unique. How about some mustaches and eye patches for the next pirate party, or pretty headbands to keep wild hair out of your face? In this chapter, you will learn how to make more complicated shapes and how to make projects that are crocheted in separate pieces and then sewn together.

Not Poisonous—Guaranteed!

A Cuddly Striped Snake

You need to know how to: make a magic loop, chain stitch, single crochet, increase, and decrease

1 Start by making a magic loop with the red yarn.

2 **Round 1:** Crochet 10 single crochets in the magic loop, then carefully pull the yarn so that the magic loop closes.

3 **Round 2:** Continuing around in a spiral, crochet 2 single crochets in each stitch of the first round. Use a scrap of yarn in a different color to mark the beginning of the round.

4 **Round 3:** Work 1 single crochet in every stitch of the previous round.

5 **Round 4:** Single crochet in the next stitch, then work 2 single crochets in the next stitch. Continue around in this pattern, increasing in every other stitch.

6 **Round 5:** Same as Round 3.

7 **Round 6:** Single crochet in the next 2 stitches, then work 2 single crochets in the next stitch. Continue around in this pattern all the way around.

8 **Round 7:** Same as Round 3.

9 **Round 8:** Single crochet in the next 3 stitches, then work 2 single crochets in the next stitch. Continue around in this pattern all the way around.

10 **Round 9:** Same as Round 3.

11 **Round 10:** Single crochet in the next 4 stitches, then work 2 single crochets in the next stitch. Continue around in this pattern all the way around.

12 **Round 11–23:** Same as Round 3.

13 **Round 24–26:** Join the lime green yarn and fasten off the red yarn. Work 3 rounds even (no increasing or decreasing) in single crochet.

Materials

- 1 skein (1.8 oz./50 g) fine (weight category 2) cotton yarn in pink
- 1 skein (1.8 oz./50 g) fine (weight category 2) cotton yarn in medium blue
- 1 skein (1.8 oz./50 g) fine (weight category 2) cotton yarn in lime green
- 1 skein (1.8 oz./50 g) fine (weight category 2) cotton yarn in navy blue
- 1 skein (1.8 oz./50 g) fine (weight category 2) cotton yarn in purple
- 3 skeins (1.8 oz./50 g each) fine (weight category 2) cotton yarn in red
- Polyester fiberfill
- 2 round black shank buttons, ¼ in. (8 mm) wide
- Scissors
- Yarn needle
- Sewing needle
- Sewing thread
- U.S. size Yy (3.0 mm) crochet hook

14 **Round 27–29:** Join the medium blue yarn and fasten off the lime green yarn. Work 3 rounds even in single crochet.

15 **Round 30–32:** Join the pink yarn and fasten off the medium blue yarn. work 3 rounds even in single crochet.

16 **Round 33–35:** Join the navy blue yarn and fasten off the pink yarn. Work 3 rounds even in single crochet.

17 **Round 36–38:** Join the purple yarn and fasten off the navy blue yarn. Work 3 rounds even in single crochet.

18 **Round 39–41:** Join the red yarn and fasten off the purple yarn. Work 3 rounds even in single crochet.

19 **Rounds 42–167:** Repeat Rounds 24–41 (steps 13–18) 7 more times. You should have 8 full sets of stripes.

20 **Round 168:** Single crochet in the next 4 stitches, then single crochet 2 together. Repeat this pattern all the way around.

21 **Rounds 169–171:** Work even in single crochet.

22 **Round 172:** Single crochet in the next 3 stitches, then single crochet 2 together. Repeat this pattern all the way around.

23 **Rounds 173–175:** Work even in single crochet.

24 **Round 176:** Single crochet in the next 2 stitches, then single crochet 2 together. Repeat this pattern all the way around.

25 Stop crocheting (but do not fasten off) and stuff your snake with fiberfill before the opening becomes too small. Roll the snake back and forth a bit as you do this so that the stuffing is evenly distributed.

26 **Rounds 177–180:** Work even in single crochet.

27 **Round 181:** Single crochet in the next stitch, then single crochet 2 together. Repeat this pattern all the way around.

28 **Rounds 182–186:** Work even in single crochet.

29 **Round 187:** Single crochet 2 together. Repeat all the way around.

30 **Rounds 188–190:** Work even in single crochet.

31 Cut the yarn about 6 in. (15 cm) from the hook and pull the end through the loop. Use your crochet hook or a yarn needle to weave the tail of yarn through all the stitches of the last round. Pull tight to close the end of the snake, then tie off the yarn and weave the tail into the fabric with a yarn needle.

TIP

The best way to get a clean transition between colors is to join the new color right before you finish the last stitch of the old color. When you have two loops left of the last stitch, yarn over with the new color and finish the stitch by pulling the yarn through the two loops.

TIP

Is your snake's long body getting in your way? Roll up the part that you have already crocheted and hold it together with a rubber band while you work on the end.

32 For the tongue, chain 13 plus 1 turning chain with lime green. Single crochet in the second chain from your hook and in each chain across. When you get to the end, turn the work.

33 Chain 1. Single crochet in the first 10 stitches, then chain 4. Turn your work and single crochet in the second chain from the hook and the next 2 chains, then in each of the 10 single crochets of the previous round. At the end of the round, fasten off by cutting the yarn and pulling the end through the loop. Use a yarn needle to weave all the ends into the fabric.

34 Use the sewing needle and thread to sew the tongue and the buttons for eyes onto the snake's head.

TIP

Instead of a striped snake, you can also crochet a single-colored snake by using just one color of yarn. You could embroider a pattern on the finished snake for some decoration. If you would like the snake to be thinner, simply work with fewer increase rounds at the beginning. If you want it to be fatter, work more increase rounds at the start. A fat snake makes a great neck pillow!

c)

Taming Wild Hair

Headbands in Fresh Colors

You need to know how to: chain stitch, slip stitch, single crochet, and double crochet

1 With the main color, chain 12, then join the last chain to the first with a slip stitch to form a ring. Make sure that your chain does not get twisted as you do this.

2 Single crochet in each chain around the ring, then continue to go around in a spiral in single crochet.

3 Check every once in a while to see if your tube is long enough to cover the headband. Our headbands needed 78 rounds of single crochet to cover them. Once the tube is long enough, slide the headband into it.

4 Cut the yarn about 6 in. (15 cm) from the crochet hook and pull the end through the loop. Close up both ends of the tube with whipstitch. Use a yarn needle to weave all the yarn ends back into the crocheted fabric.

Materials

Blue Headband

- 1 skein (1.8 oz./50 g) fine (weight category 2) cotton yarn in blue
- Small amount of fine (weight category 2) cotton yarn in white
- Small amount of fine (weight category 2) cotton yarn in red
- 1 white flower-shaped button
- Plastic headband, about ½ in. (1 cm) wide
- U.S. size yy (3.0 mm) crochet hook)
- Fabric glue
- Craft glue
- Yarn needle
- Scissors

Purple Headband

- 1 skein (1.8 oz./50 g) fine (weight category 2) cotton yarn in purple
- Small amount of fine (weight category 2) cotton yarn in orange
- Small amount of fine (weight category 2) cotton yarn in pink
- 1 white flower-shaped button
- Plastic headband, about ½ in. (1 cm) wide
- U.S. size yy (3.0 mm) crochet hook)
- Fabric glue
- Craft glue
- Yarn needle
- Scissors

5 For decorative wavy lines, chain 120. Check to make sure it's long enough to decorate the headband in the pattern you want, then fasten off the chain. Weave the tails at the beginning and end into the chain.

6 For the flower, chain 6, then then join the last chain to the first with a slip stitch to form a ring.

7 Work 15 single crochets into the ring; at the end, join the last stitch to the first one with a slip stitch.

8 Chain 3, then work 3 double crochets in the next stitch.

9 Chain 3, then slip stitch in the next stitch to form the end of this petal.

10 Single crochet in the next stitch.

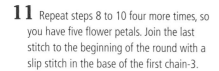

11 Repeat steps 8 to 10 four more times, so you have five flower petals. Join the last stitch to the beginning of the round with a slip stitch in the base of the first chain-3.

12 Cut the yarn and pull the end through the loop. Weave the end into the fabric. Your flower is finished.

13 Glue the chain you made in step 5 to the headband with fabric glue.

14 Next, glue the flower to the headband, on top of the chain, with fabric glue. Let everything dry, then glue the button on in the center of the flower with craft glue.

TIP

The flower is the only part of this project that uses double crochet. If you haven't learned double crochet yet, you can still make the headband—just decorate it with cute buttons or a ribbon tied in a bow.

Slouchy Beret

A Stylish Hat Trimmed with a Little Bow

You need to know how to: chain stitch, slip stitch, single crochet, and double crochet

Materials

❀ 2 skeins (1.8 oz./50 g each) light (weight category 3) acrylic yarn in purple

❀ Small amount of fine (weight category 2) cotton yarn in aqua

❀ 1 pink flower-shaped button, about ½ in. (15 mm) wide

❀ U.S. size yy (3.5 mm) crochet hook

❀ Scissors

❀ Yarn needle

1 With purple, chain 7, then join the last chain to the first with a slip stitch to form a ring.

2 Round 1: Chain 3, then work 9 double crochets through the ring. Join the end of the round to the beginning by working a slip stitch in the top stitch of the beginning chain-3.

3 Round 2: Chain 4. In the next double crochet of the previous round, work 1 double crochet, chain 1, then work another double crochet in the same stitch, then chain 1.

4 In the next stitch, double crochet, chain 1, double crochet in the same stitch, then chain 1. Repeat this in every stitch around the piece.

5 Join the end of the round to the beginning by working a slip stitch in the third chain of the beginning 4 chains.

6 Round 3: Chain 4. Work 1 double crochet in the next chain space of the previous round (the chain between the slip stitch at the end of the round and the first double crochet of the round), inserting the hook into the space *underneath* the chain, not into the chain itself. Chain 1.

7 In the next chain space, double crochet, chain 1, double crochet in the same space, and chain 1. Repeat this in every chain space around the piece. Join the end of the round to the beginning by working a slip stitch in the third chain of the beginning 4 chains.

8 Round 4: Chain 4. Work 1 double crochet in the next chain space of the previous round, then chain 1.

9 In the next chain space, double crochet, chain 1, double crochet again in the same chain space, and chain 1. Double crochet in the next chain space, then chain 1. Repeat this pattern around the piece, working 2 double crochet in every other chain space, always with 1 chain in between. Join the end of the round to the beginning by working a slip stitch in the third chain of the beginning 4 chains.

10 Round 5: Chain 4. Double crochet in the first chain space, then chain 1.

11 Double crochet in the next chain space, chain 1. Repeat this pattern around the piece. Join the end of the round to the beginning by working a slip stitch in the third chain of the beginning chain-4.

12 **Round 6:** Chain 4. Double crochet in the next chain space, then chain 1, then double crochet in the next chain space and chain 1. In the third chain space, double crochet, chain 1, then double crochet in the same chain space again, and chain 1. Repeat this pattern around the piece.

13 Join the end of the round to the beginning by working a slip stitch in the third chain of the beginning 4 chains.

14 **Round 7:** Chain 4. Double crochet in next chain space, then chain 1. Repeat this pattern around the piece. Join the end of the round to the beginning by working a slip stitch in the third chain of the beginning 4 chains.

15 **Rounds 8–16:** Same as Round 7.

16 **Round 17:** Chain 2. Single crochet in the next chain space, then chain 1. Repeat in this pattern around the piece. Join the end of the round to the beginning by working a slip stitch in the first chain.

17 **Rounds 18–22:** Same as Round 17.

18 Cut the yarn about 6 in. (15 cm) from the hook and pull the end through the loop. Pull the knot tight. Use a yarn needle to weave in the beginning and ending tails.

19 For the bow, chain 14, plus 1 turning chain, with aqua.

20 Single crochet in the second chain from the hook and in each chain across. When you get to the end, turn the work.

21 Chain 1. Single crochet in each stitch across. Turn.

22 Repeat step 21 eleven more times until you have a little rectangle. Fasten off and use a yarn needle to weave the beginning and ending tails into the fabric.

23 Fold the little square like an accordion and wrap a piece of yarn around the middle. Pull it tight, then tie it off to hold the bow in shape.

24 Sew the button to the bow and the bow to the brim of the hat at the same time, making sure to go through all layers with each stitch.

25 Your hat is finished!

TIP

You can also glue or sew the bow to a pin back and pin it to the hat. You could even make a lot of little bows and flowers on pins so you can switch in whichever decoration you feel like wearing that day!

Pretty Coasters

Granny Squares in a Circle

You need to know how to: chain stitch, slip stitch, single crochet, and double crochet

Materials

- 1 skein (1.8 oz./50 g) fine (weight category 2) cotton yarn in purple
- 1 skein (1.8 oz./50 g) fine (weight category 2) cotton yarn in green
- 1 skein (1.8 oz./50 g) fine (weight category 2) cotton yarn in magenta
- U.S. size YY (4.0 mm) crochet hook
- Scissors
- Yarn needle
- Old towel
- Straight pins
- Spray bottle

1 With purple, chain 6, then join the last chain to the first with a slip stitch to form a ring.

2 **Round 1:** Chain 4 (counts as first double crochet + 1 chain). Double crochet through the ring, then chain 1; repeat this 10 more times until you have 12 double crochets (counting the beginning chain). Join the round with a slip stitch in the third chain of the beginning chain-4. Fasten off by cutting the yarn about 4 in. (10 cm) from the hook and pulling the end through the loop.

3 **Round 2:** Join the green yarn in any chain space and chain 3 (counts as first double crochet). In the same chain space, work 2 more double crochets, inserting the hook under the chain instead of through it. Chain 1. [In the next chain space, work 3 double crochets, then chain 1.] Repeat the instruction in the brackets in each chain space all the way around the piece. Join the round with a slip stitch in the third chain of the beginning chain-3. Fasten off.

4 **Round 3:** Same as Round 2, but with magenta yarn.

5 **Round 4:** Join the purple yarn in any chain space; chain 1, then work 1 single crochet in that chain space. [Chain 4, then work 1 single crochet in the next chain space.] Repeat the instructions in brackets all the way around the coaster. Join the round with a slip stitch in the beginning chain. Fasten off.

6 Hide all the tails of yarn by weaving them into the coaster with a yarn needle.

7 Wet block your coaster so it lies flat and even (see page 25).

Spring Flower Garlands

Always Fresh!

You need to know how to: chain stitch, slip stitch, single crochet, half double crochet, double crochet, treble crochet, and sew

1 Start with a magic loop in pink.

2 Chain 3, then work 2 double crochets through the magic loop.

3 Chain 3, then work a slip stitch through the magic loop. Your first flower petal is finished.

4 Repeat steps 2 and 3 four more times for a total of 5 flower petals.

5 Cut the yarn about 4 in. (10 cm) from the crochet hook and pull the end through the loop. Carefully pull on the starting end to close the magic loop. Use a yarn needle to weave the starting and ending tails into the stitches.

6 Crochet nine more flowers as described in steps 1 to 5.

7 For the leaves, chain 9 (8 foundation chains plus 1 turning chain) with green.

8 Single crochet in the second chain from the hook. Half double crochet in the next 2 chains. Double crochet in the next 2 chains. Treble crochet in the next 2 chains. You should have 1 chain left at this point.

9 In the last chain, work 5 double crochets. These stitches will curve out around the end of the chain so you can keep crocheting along the back of the chain.

10 Working in the unused loops along the back of the chain, skip the end chain (the one with 5 double crochets in it already) and treble crochet in the next 2 chains. Double crochet in the next 2 chains. Half double crochet in the next 2 chains. Single crochet in the last chain. Now you are back at the tip of the leaf.

11 Work a slip stitch in the turning chain at the very tip of the leaf, then cut the yarn about 4 in. (10 cm) from the hook and pull the end through the loop. Use a yarn needle to weave the starting and ending tails of yarn into the leaf.

12 Crochet 21 more leaves as described in steps 7 to 11.

13 For the vine, chain 221 with the green yarn.

14 Single crochet in the second chain from the hook and in each chain across. Fasten off and weave in the starting and ending tails.

15 Wet block all of the pieces to make them even and flat (see page 25).

16 Sew the leaves and flowers securely onto the crocheted vine. For each piece, come up through the vine, then up through the flower or leaf, take the yarn through a bead in the matching color, then go back down through the flower or leaf and vine. Take one more stitch through all the parts in the same way, then tie the beginning and ending tails together on the back of the vine. For a garland like ours, start about 4 in. (10 cm) from the beginning with a pair of leaves, and alternate between two leaves and one flower, spacing out every set of three pieces over about 20 stitches.

TIP

This garland is a great decoration for door-frames and bulletin boards. You could also make a shorter one and wear it in your hair or use it to trim a picture frame.

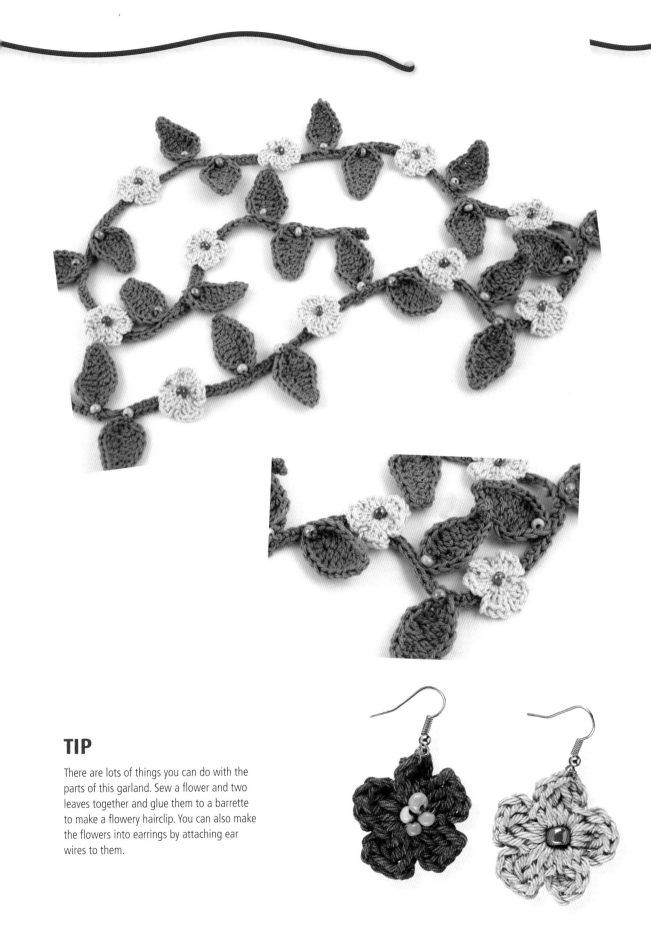

TIP

There are lots of things you can do with the parts of this garland. Sew a flower and two leaves together and glue them to a barrette to make a flowery hairclip. You can also make the flowers into earrings by attaching ear wires to them.

Ahoy, Mateys!
swashbuckling Mustaches and Eye Patches

You need to know how to: chain stitch, single crochet, half double crochet, double crochet, treble crochet, and decrease

Pirate Mustaches

There are really two patterns here: One for a regular mustache and one for an extra-curly mustache (in red in the picture on the next page). The instructions for the extra-curly version are given in parentheses after the regular instructions; to follow the regular instructions, ignore the numbers in parentheses. The follow the extra-curly instructions, every time you come to parentheses, ignore the first number and use the one in the parentheses. So for the regular mustache, you will start by chaining 27, and for the extra-curly one you will chain 31.

1 Start with a slip knot.

2 Chain 27 (31).

3 Row 1: Single crochet in the second chain from the hook. In the next 2 chains, single crochet 2 together.

4 (Extra-curly version: Single crochet in the next 3 chains.) In the next 2 chains, single crochet 2 together.

5 Half double crochet in the next 2 chains. Double crochet in the next 2 chains. Treble crochet in the next 3 chains.

6 Chain 3, then slip stitch in the next chain.

7 Single crochet in the next chain. This is the middle of your mustache.

Materials
Pirate Mustaches
- Small amount of medium (weight category 4) wool-acrylic blend yarn in yellow or red
- U.S. size YY (3.5 mm) crochet hook
- Scissors
- Yarn needle
- Old towel
- Straight pins
- Spray bottle

8 Now work the second half of the mustache as a mirror image of the first half. Start by chaining 3.

9 Treble crochet in the next 3 chains, double crochet in the next 2 chains, half double crochet in the next 2 chains.

10 In the next 2 chains, single crochet 2 together. (Single crochet in the next 3 chains.) Single crochet 2 together again, then single crochet in the last chain.

11 Cut the yarn about 4 in. (10 cm) away from the crochet hook and pull the end through the loop. Use a yarn needle to weave in the starting and ending yarn tails.

12 If your mustache won't lie flat, you can wet block it (see page 25).

TIP

You can glue your mustache to bags, post-cards, or your shoes, sew it onto a pin back, or attach it with double-sided tape to your upper lip.

You need to know how to: chain stitch, single crochet, and decrease

Eye Patches

1 Chain 113.

2 Single crochet in the second chain from the hook and in the next 62 chains.

3 Turn your work.

4 Chain 1. Single crochet in the next 15 stitches. Turn.

5 Repeat step 4 five times.

7 Repeat step 6 until only 3 stitches are left.

8 Work one last row of single crochet, this time without decreasing at all.

9 At the end of this last row, chain 1, but do not turn. Continue to crochet down the side of the eye patch, alternating 1 single crochet in the end of a row and 1 chain stitch until you reach the part of the foundation chain with no single crochets.

Materials

Eye Patches

❀ Small amount of medium (weight category 4) wool-acrylic blend yarn in blue or red

❀ U.S. size YY (3.5 mm) crochet hook

❀ Scissors

❀ Yarn needle

❀ Old towel

❀ Straight pins

❀ Spray bottle

10 When you get to the foundation chain, single crochet in each chain to the end. Fasten off the yarn. Use a yarn needle to weave in the tails at both ends.

6 In the next row, chain 1, then single crochet the first 2 stitches together. Single crochet across the row (working 1 single crochet in each stitch) until you reach the last 2 stitches; single crochet the last 2 stitches together. Turn.

11 Wet block the eye patch to flatten it out (see page 25). Then tie it on and have an adventure!

Personalize It!

Decorate Your Clothing with Crocheted Details

You need to know how to: make a magic loop, chain stitch, slip stitch, single crochet, half double crochet, double crochet, and treble crochet

Star Shirt

Big Star

1 Start with a magic loop.

2 Round 1: Chain 3, then work 14 double crochet through the loop. Join the last stitch to the beginning of the round by working a slip stitch in the third chain of the beginning chain-3. Pull on the starting yarn to tighten the loop.

3 Round 2: Chain 5. Single crochet in the second chain from the hook.

4 Half double crochet in the next chain; double crochet in the next chain; treble crochet in the last chain. This forms a star point.

5 Connect this side of the star point with the center of the star by working a slip stitch in the third double crochet after the stitch the chain-5 was connected to. (Each of the five points around the star spans 3 stitches of the center round.)

6 Repeat steps 3 to 5 four times, to make a total of five star points. You will work the last slip stitch in the top of the beginning chain-3 of Round 1, where the first chain-5 of Round 2 starts. Cut the yarn about 4 in. (10 cm) from the hook and pull the end through the loop. Use a yarn needle to weave in the starting and ending tails of yarn.

Materials

star shirt

- ❀ Navy blue long-sleeve T-shirt in your size
- ❀ 1 skein (1.8 oz/50 g) of fine (weight category 2) cotton yarn in medium blue
- ❀ 1 skein (1.8 oz/50 g) of fine (weight category 2) cotton yarn in white
- ❀ 1 skein (1.8 oz/50 g) of fine (weight category 2) cotton yarn in red
- ❀ 1 skein (1.8 oz/50 g) of fine (weight category 2) cotton yarn in pink
- ❀ U.S. size YY (3.0 mm) crochet hook
- ❀ Scissors
- ❀ Yarn needle
- ❀ Fusible web or iron-on--patch kit
- ❀ Parchment paper
- ❀ Pins with glass or metal heads
- ❀ Iron
- ❀ Ironing board or old towel

Medium Star

1 Start with a magic loop.

2 **Round 1:** Chain 3, then work 11 double crochet through the loop. Join the last stitch to the beginning of the round by working a slip stitch in the third chain of the beginning chain-3. Pull on the starting yarn to tighten the loop.

3 **Round 2:** Chain 4. Single crochet in the second chain from the hook; half double crochet in the next chain; double crochet in the last chain. This forms a star point.

4 Connect this side of the star point with the center of the star by working a slip stitch in the next double crochet of Round 1. (The first round has 12 stitches, counting the first chain-3, so the points on this star will not be spaced exactly evenly. Just connect each point to the stitch that it falls closest to.)

5 Repeat steps 3 and 4 four times, to make a total of five star points. You will work the last slip stitch in the top of the beginning chain-3 of Round 1, where the first chain-4 of Round 2 starts. Cut the yarn about 4 in. (10 cm) from the hook and pull the end through the loop. Use a yarn needle to weave in the starting and ending tails of yarn.

Making a Star Shirt

To make your star shirt, crochet several stars in your choice of sizes and colors. Use the fusible web or iron-on–patch kit to iron them onto the shirt, following the manufacturer's instructions. Have an adult help you with this part.

Little Star

1 Start with a magic loop.

2 **Round 1:** Chain 3, then work 8 double crochet through the loop. Join the last stitch to the beginning of the round by working a slip stitch in the third chain of the beginning chain-3. Pull on the starting yarn to tighten the loop.

3 **Round 2:** Chain 3. Single crochet in the second chain from the hook; half double crochet in the last chain. This forms a star point.

4 Connect this side of the star point with the center of the star by working a slip stitch in the next double crochet after the stitch the chain-4 was connected to. (The first round has 9 stitches, counting the first chain-3, so the points on this star will not be spaced exactly evenly. Just connect each point to the stitch that it falls closest to.)

5 Repeat steps 3 and 4 four times, to make a total of five star points. You will work the last slip stitch in the top of the beginning chain-3 of Round 1, where the first chain-4 of Round 2 starts. Cut the yarn about 4 in. (10 cm) from the hook and pull the end through the loop. Use a yarn needle to weave in the starting and ending tails of yarn.

Scarf with Crocheted Buttons

1 Start with a magic loop.

2 **Round 1:** Chain 3, then work 9 double crochet through the loop. Join the last stitch to the beginning of the round by working a slip stitch in the third chain of the beginning chain-3. Pull on the starting yarn to tighten the loop.

3 Cut the yarn about 4 in. (10 cm) from the hook and pull the end through the loop. Use a yarn needle to weave in the starting and ending tails of yarn.

4 Make seven circles in each color in this way. Sew the buttons to the edge of the scarf, using yarn in different colors, by sewing a large cross in the center of each button and then tying off the yarn on the back.

You need to know how to: make a magic loop, chain stitch, slip stitch, single crochet, double crochet, increase, decrease, and sew

Owl shirt

1 Start with a magic loop in lime green.

2 **Round 1:** Chain 3, then work 11 double crochets through the loop. Join the last stitch to the beginning of the round by working a slip stitch in the third chain of the beginning chain-3. Pull on the starting yarn to tighten the loop.

3 **Round 2:** Chain 3, then work 1 double crochet in the top of the beginning chain-3 of the previous round (where you put the slip stitch). Work 2 double crochets in each stitch around the piece. Join the last stitch to the beginning of the round by working a slip stitch in the third chain of the beginning chain-3. Fasten off by cutting the yarn about 4 in. (10 cm) from the hook and pulling the end through the loop.

4 **Round 3:** Join the magenta yarn in any stitch and chain 1. Single crochet in the next stitch, then work 2 single crochets in the next stitch. Continue in this pattern around the piece, increasing in every other stitch. Fasten off.

5 **Round 4:** Join the purple yarn in any stitch. Chain 3. Double crochet in the same stitch as joining. [Double crochet in the next 2 stitches, then work 2 double crochets in the next stitch.] Repeat the instructions in brackets around the whole piece. Join the last stitch to the beginning of the round by working a slip stitch in the third chain of the beginning chain-3. Turn your work.

6 **Row 5:** Chain 3. Double crochet 2 together in the next 2 stitches, then double crochet in the next 11 stitches, then double crochet 2 together again in the next 2 stitches. Turn your work.

7 **Row 6:** Chain 3. Double crochet in each stitch of the last row. Turn your work.

8 **Row 7:** Chain 3, then single crochet in the second chain from the hook and half double crochet in the next chain. This will make a little triangle.

9 Join the end of the triangle to the owl's head by working a slip stitch in the stitch after the next one.

10 Single crochet in the next 8 stitches.

11 Repeat steps 8 and 9 to make another ear.

12 Fasten off. Use a yarn needle to weave all the tails into the stitches of the same color.

Materials

Owl shirt

- White long-sleeve T-shirt in your size
- 1 skein (1.8 oz/50 g) of fine (weight category 2) cotton yarn in lime green
- 1 skein (1.8 oz/50 g) of fine (weight category 2) cotton yarn in magenta
- 1 skein (1.8 oz/50 g) of fine (weight category 2) cotton yarn in purple
- 1 skein (1.8 oz/50 g) of fine (weight category 2) cotton yarn in white
- 1 skein (1.8 oz/50 g) of fine (weight category 2) cotton yarn in aqua
- Small amount of fine (weight category 2) cotton yarn in orange
- Black permanent felt-tip marker
- U.S. size YY (3.0 mm) crochet hook
- Scissors
- Yarn needle
- Old towel
- Straight pins with metal or glass heads
- Spray bottle
- Fusible web or iron-on–patch kit
- Parchment paper
- Iron
- Ironing board

13 With white, make a magic loop. Chain 3, then work 11 double crochets through the loop. Join the last stitch to the beginning of the round by working a slip stitch in the third chain of the beginning chain-3. Pull on the starting yarn to tighten the loop. Fasten off. Make another eye just like the first. Sew the eyes to the owl's head with a yarn needle and white yarn.

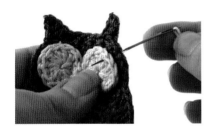

14 With orange yarn, sew the owl's beak by making lots of stitches over the same area.

15 Repeat step 13 with the aqua yarn to make 8 circles.

16 Color in the pupils of the owl's eyes with the permanent marker. Wet block the pieces so they'll lie flat, then use the fusible web or iron-on–patch kit to attach them to the T-shirt, following the manufacturer's instructions.

Butterfly Collection

Add Color to Your Walls

You need to know how to: make a magic loop, chain stitch, slip stitch, single crochet, half double crochet, double crochet, and treble crochet

1 Start with a slip knot in the wing color.

2 Chain 4. Double crochet in the third chain from your hook. This chain will be the middle of the butterfly's body, and all the wings will be worked through this chain. In these instructions, we will call this chain the base chain. Chain 3, then work a slip stitch in the base chain.

3 Chain 4. Work 3 treble crochets in the base chain. Chain 4, then work a slip stitch in the base chain.

4 Repeat step 3 to make another big wing.

Materials

- Small amount of fine (weight category 2) cotton yarn in various colors (2 colors for each butterfly)
- 18 beads in various colors (2 matching beads for each butterfly), ¼ in. (0.5 cm) wide
- Deep picture frame, 10 by 10 in. (25 by 25 cm), with a wide mat
- Corrugated cardboard
- 18 straight pins
- Decorative paper
- Craft glue
- Glue stick
- U.S. size YY (3.0 mm) crochet hook
- Scissors
- Yarn needle
- Pencil

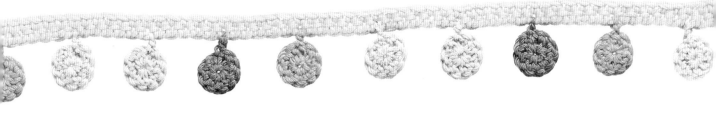

5 For the last (small) wing, chain 3, work 2 double crochets in the base chain, chain 3 again, then work a slip stitch in the base chain.

6 Cut the yarn 4 in. (10 cm) from the hook and pull the end through the loop. Use a yarn needle to weave in the tails.

7 With the body and antennae color, chain 3.

8 Insert the hook through the base chain from the front of the body to the back, with the yarn going between the two big wings and around to the back. Yarn over and pull up a loop through the middle of the butterfly.

9 Now bring the yarn around the back and up between the two small wings. Yarn over and pull through both loops on the hook, as if you were crocheting a single crochet around and through the butterfly.

10 Chain 8, then wrap this chain around the other side of the butterfly so that it goes up the center between the wings.

11 Slip stitch through the very top of the butterfly to hold the chain in place.

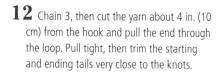

12 Chain 3, then cut the yarn about 4 in. (10 cm) from the hook and pull the end through the loop. Pull tight, then trim the starting and ending tails very close to the knots.

13 Repeat steps 1–12 eight more times, for a total of nine butterflies. Use whatever color combinations you like.

14 Glue the beads to the large wings of the butterflies so that the holes are pointing up.

15 To mount your butterfly collection, first take the mat out of the frame. Trace the outline of the inner window on the cardboard, then on the decorative paper.

16 Cut the square out of the cardboard and paper. Use the glue stitck to glue the paper to the cardboard.

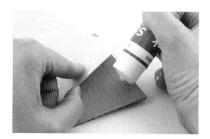

17 Put the decorated cardboard inside the mat and glue everything to the backing of the frame.

18 Use the pencil to lightly mark nine dots evenly spaced out in a square on the decorated paper.

19 Use one or two pins to stick each butterfly right above a mark.

20 Put the front of the frame on, then hang your collection.

TIP

You can decorate the butterflies by crocheting around the wings in slip stitch with a different color before you put the bodies on or by gluing buttons or sequins to the wings. You can also use these butterflies to decorate a postcard or a notebook.

Projects for Pros

Have you mastered the projects and skills in the first two chapters? Then it's time for some more challenging projects where you'll learn some new skills. How about a blanket with a decorative border, a fringed scarf, or some multi-colored fingerless mitts that introduce new stitches? The cuddly cat at the end of the book, in addition to being adorable, will help you learn to crochet a project in several pieces and then sew them together.

Have fun!

Warm Up

A Cozy Striped Blanket

You need to know how to: chain stitch, slip stitches, single crochet, and double crochet

You'll learn how to: crochet a shell stitch border

Materials

- 2 skeins (1.8 oz./50 g each) light (weight category 3) wool-acrylic blend yarn in magenta
- 2 skeins (1.8 oz./50 g each) light (weight category 3) wool-acrylic blend yarn in medium blue
- 2 skeins (1.8 oz./50 g each) light (weight category 3) wool-acrylic blend yarn in light pink
- 2 skeins (1.8 oz./50 g each) light (weight category 3) wool-acrylic blend yarn in maroon
- 2 skeins (1.8 oz./50 g each) light (weight category 3) wool-acrylic blend yarn in aqua
- 2 skeins (1.8 oz./50 g each) light (weight category 3) wool-acrylic blend yarn in navy blue
- 2 skeins (1.8 oz./50 g each) light (weight category 3) wool-acrylic blend yarn in medium pink
- 1 skein (3.5 oz/100 g) light (weight category 3) wool-acrylic blend yarn in bright blue
- U.S. size YY (4.0 mm) crochet hook
- Scissors
- Yarn needle

1 With magenta, chain 207.

2 **Row 1:** Double crochet in the 8th chain from the hook and in the next chain. [Chain 2, skip next 2 chains, double crochet in next 2 chains.] Repeat the instructions in brackets across the whole row. Double crochet in the last chain. Turn.

3 **Row 2:** Chain 3. Double crochet in the chain space immediately below, inserting the hook underneath the chain, not through it. [Chain 2, skip next 2 stitches, work 2 double crochets in next chain space.] Repeat the instructions in brackets across the whole row. Turn.

4 **Row 3:** Cut the yarn and join the next color in the stripe pattern (see step 5). Chain 5. [Skip next 2 stitches, work 2 double crochets in the next chain space, chain 2.] Repeat the instructions in brackets across the row. Work 1 double crochet in the top of the beginning chain-3 of the previous row. Turn.

5 Work the next row the same as Row 2. Continue to alternate Row 2 and 3, changing colors to follow this strip sequence: 2 rows magenta, 2 rows medium blue, 2 rows light pink, 2 rows maroon, 2 rows aqua, 2 rows navy blue, 2 rows medium pink.

6 Go through this stripe sequence over and over until you have used every color 10 times.

7 Cut the yarn about 6 in. (15 cm) from the hook and pull the end through the loop.

8 Use a yarn needle to weave all the tails of yarn into the stitches of the same color.

9 For the border, join the bright blue yarn at the right side of the top edge of the blanket. Work 1 single crochet in every stitch and 2 single crochets in every chain space across the top of the blanket. When you get to the corner, work 3 single crochets in the corner stitch to go around the corner, then continue down the side of the blanket. Work 2 single crochets around each double crochet (which are now sideways) or beginning chain-3.

10 Work 3 single crochets in the next corner stitch and continue across the bottom, working 1 single crochet in the unused loops of each chain stitch. Go around the corner and up the other side of the blanket in the same way as before. When you get to where you started, work 2 more single crochets in the corner stitch (for a total of 3) and then join to the first stitch with a slip stitch.

11 Now you'll crochet a round of shell stitch. To make a shell: [Skip 1 stitch, work 5 double crochets in the next stitch, skip 1 stitch, single crochet in the next stitch.] Repeat the instructions in brackets all the way around the edge of the blanket. Join to the beginning of the round with a slip stitch and fasten off.

12 Weave in the beginning and ending tails with a yarn needle.

TIP

This blanket is very quick and easy to make, so you could even make a much bigger one that you could use as a bedspread.

TIP

Do you have a lot of leftover yarn? This blanket is a great way to use it up! Get creative with the stripe pattern, using any colors you want in any order. Any combination looks great!

TIP

You can also work the pattern in rounds instead of in rows. This makes a great infinity scarf. To do this, start with a somewhat shorter chain (depending on how long you want the scarf to be) and join it into a ring with a slip stitch. Crochet the pattern crochet round by round, as described, and stop when the scarf is tall enough.

Fringed Scarf

Materials

- 1 skein (1.8 oz./50 g) medium (weight category 4) wool-acrylic blend yarn in pink
- 1 skein (1.8 oz./50 g) medium (weight category 4) wool-acrylic blend yarn in purple
- 1 skein (1.8 oz./50 g) medium (weight category 4) wool-acrylic blend yarn in green
- 1 skein (1.8 oz./50 g) medium (weight category 4) wool-acrylic blend yarn in red
- U.S. size YY (4.0 mm) crochet hook
- Scissors
- Yarn needle
- Piece of stiff cardboard

In Fresh Spring Colors

You need to know how to: chain stitch, slip stitch, and double crochet

You'll learn how to: make a fringe

1 With red, chain 30.

2 Row 1: Work 4 double crochets in the 6th chain from the hook.

3 [Skip 3 chains, then work 4 double crochets in the next chain.] Repeat the instructions in brackets across the row.

4 Work 1 double crochet in the last chain. Turn.

5 Row 2: Chain 3 (counts as first double crochet). Work 3 double crochets in the space between the last stitch and the last set of 4 double crochets of the row below, inserting the hook through the space, not through any of the stitches. [Work 4 double crochets in the next space between 4-double-crochet clusters.] Repeat the instructions in brackets across the row. When you get to the end of the row, work 4 double crochets in the chain loop at the beginning of the first row. Turn.

6 **Row 3:** Cut the old yarn and join the next color in the stripe pattern (see step 9). Chain 3.

7 [Work 4 double crochets in the next space between 4-double-crochet clusters.] Repeat the instructions in brackets across the row. When you get to the end of the row, double crochet in the top of the beginning chain-3 of the previous row. Turn.

8 **Row 4:** Chain 3 (counts as first double crochet). Work 3 double crochets in the space between the last stitch and the last set of 4 double crochets of the previous row. [Work 4 double crochets in the next space between 4-double-crochet clusters.] Repeat the instructions in brackets across the row. When you get to the end of the row, work 4 double crochets in the space between the last 4-double-crochet cluster and the beginning chain-3 of the previous row. Turn.

9 Repeat Rows 3 and 4, changing colors to follow this stripe pattern: 2 rows of red, 2 rows of purple, 2 rows of green, 2 rows of pink.

10 Repeat the stripe pattern until the scarf is as long as you want it to be. (In our scarf, each color is used 12 times.) Fasten off.

11 Use a yarn needle to weave all the tails of yarn into the stitches of the same color.

12 For the fringes, cut a piece of cardboard about 6 in. (15 cm) wide and wrap each color of yarn around it about five times.

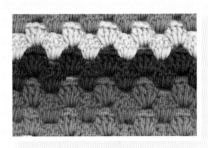

13 Cut the wrapped threads on one side. This will give you four bunches of yarn all the same length.

14 Take one bunch and pull it through a hole along a short edge of the scarf. You can do this with your fingers or with a big crochet hook.

15 Pull the ends of the yarn through the loop formed and pull tight to knot them around the edge of the scarf. Repeat these steps to add bundles of fringe to each gap along both ends of the scarf.

16 If needed, trim the fringe so it's all the same length.

TIP

There are a lot of tails to weave in in this scarf! To avoid so much weaving in, you can make the scarf all in one color or crochet it sideways, with long stripes. For the sideways version, start with 403 chains, and work only 2 rows of each color before fastening off the work.

Cool Shoulder Bag

Lots of Space for Books and Clothes

You need to know how to: chain stitch, slip stitch, single crochet, and double crochet

1 With purple, chain 63.

2 **Round 1:** Double crochet in the 4th chain from the hook. Double crochet in each remaining chain to the end of the row.

3 When you get to the end of the row, work 3 double crochets in the last chain stitch to go around the end.

4 Now double crochet back across the other side of the chain. Work the stitches in the spaces in between the stitches on the first side, instead of in the chain itself.

5 At the end of the row, work 3 double crochets in the last chain. Join the last stitch to the top of the beginning 3 chains with a slip stitch.

6 **Round 2:** Chain 3. Double crochet in the space between stitches below (insert the hook between the stitches, not through a stitch). Double crochet in each space around. Join the end with a slip stitch in the third chain of the beginning chain-3.

7 **Round 3–5:** Same as Round 2.

8 **Round 6:** Join the blue yarn and cut the purple yarn. Single crochet in the space between stitches, then chain 3. [Skip 2 spaces and single crochet in the next space. Chain 3.] Repeat the instructions in brackets around the piece. Join the final chain-3 to the first single crochet with a slip stitch.

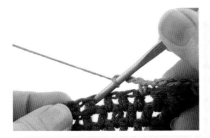

9 **Round 7:** Chain 3. Double crochet in each chain and single crochet around the purse. Join the last stitch to the third chain of the beginning chain-3 with a slip stitch.

10 **Round 8:** Join the next stripe color (see step 13) and cut off the old color. Chain 3, then single crochet in the gap between the second and third double crochets of the previous round. [Chain 3, skip 4 stitches, single crochet in the gap between the next 2 stitches.] Repeat the instructions in brackets around the piece so that there are 4 double crochets between each pair of single crochets and the single crochets are offset from the ones in Round 6. Join the end of the round to the beginning chain with a slip stitch.

11 **Round 9:** Same as Round 7.

12 **Round 10:** Join the next stripe color (see step 13) and single crochet in the next stitch. [Chain 3, skip 4 stitches, single crochet in the gap between the next 2 stitches.] Repeat the instructions in brackets around the piece so that there are 4 double crochets between each pair of single crochets and the single crochets are offset from the ones in Round 8. Join the end of the round to the beginning chain with a slip stitch.

13 **Rounds 11–19:** Repeat Rounds 7 to 10. Work the stripes in this order: Blue, bright pink, light pink. After Round 19 you should have four stripes of every color.

Materials

- 2 skeins (1.8 oz./50 g each) light (weight category 3) wool-acrylic blend yarn in purple
- 1 skein (3.5 oz/100 g) light (weight category 3) wool-acrylic blend yarn in bright blue
- 1 skein (3.5 oz/100 g) light (weight category 3) wool-acrylic blend yarn in bright pink
- 1 skein (3.5 oz/100 g) light (weight category 3) wool-acrylic blend yarn in pink
- U.S. size YY (3.5 mm) crochet hook
- Scissors
- Yarn needle

14 **Round 20:** Join the purple yarn and cut the light pink yarn. Chain 3. Double crochet in the next 2 spaces between stitches. [Skip the next space, then double crochet in the next 3 spaces.] Repeat the instructions in brackets around the piece. At the end, join with a slip stitch in the third chain of the beginning chain-3.

15 **Rounds 21–23:** Chain 3, double crochet in each space between stitches around the piece. Join with a slip stitch in the third chain of the beginning chain-3.

16 **Strap Row 1:** Chain 4, then turn your work. [Skip 1 space, double crochet in next space, chain 1.] Repeat the instructions in brackets 4 more times. Skip 1 space and work 1 more double crochet in the next space.

17 **Row 2:** Chain 4, turn. Double crochet in chain space below. [Chain 1, double crochet in next space.] Repeat the instructions in brackets to the end of the strap (5 more times).

18 Repeat Row 2 about 90 times, or until the strap is as long as you would like it to be.

19 Line the end of the strap up with the edge of the bag on the opposite side from the base of the strap. Work a row of single crochet through both pieces at the same time to join the strap to the bag.

20 Cut the yarn about 6 in. (15 cm) away from the crochet hook and pull the end through the loop. Use a yarn needle to weave all the ends of yarn into the stitches of the same color.

TIP

You can decorate your bag by gluing or sewing buttons onto it or by threading a ribbon through the upper edge.

TIP

If you're going to carry small things in your bag, you might want to add a lining. Trace your bag onto a piece of matching fabric and cut out two pieces a little bit larger than the rectangular part of the bag. Place the pieces with right sides together and sew around the sides and bottom edge. Fold the top edge down about ½ in. (13 mm) and sew around to hold the hem in place. Slip the lining inside the bag and sew the top edges of the lining and the bag together with small stitches.

Wristbands and Fingerless Mitts

Keep Your Hands Warm

You need to know how to: make a magic loop, slip stitch, chain stitch, single crochet, half double crochet, double crochet, and treble crochet

You'll learn how to: crochet through the back loop

Wristbands

1 With the main color and the larger hook, chain 11.

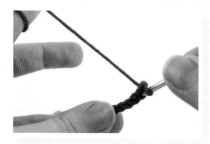

2 **Row 1:** Single crochet in the second chain and each chain across. Turn.

3 **Row 2:** Chain 1. Single crochet through the back loop in each stitch across. Turn.

Here's how: Look at the stitches of the previous row. See how each stitch is made up of two strands of yarn that form a V shape? Usually, you would insert the hook under both strands of yarn when you crochet a stitch. To work through the back loop, skip the strand in front and only insert the hook under the back strand. Finish the stitch as normal.

Working through the back loop makes a ridge along the crocheted row.

4 **Row 3:** Chain 1. Single crochet in each stitch across.

5 Repeat Rows 2 and 3 about 15 times—until the wristband is the right length. End with a Row 3.

6 Place the ends of your wristband together with the ridges on the outside and crochet the last row together with the foundation chain. To do this, chain 1, then insert your hook through the back loop of the first stitch and through the unused loop at the bottom of the foundation chain at the same time. Work a single crochet as normal. Do the same in each stitch across.

7 Cut the yarn about 6 in. (15 cm) from the hook and pull the end through the loop. Use a yarn needle to weave the tails into the stitches.

Star

These instructions are the same as the ones for the medium star for the star shirt (page 93). If you find the instructions tricky, take a look at the photos for crocheting the large star on page 92.

1 Start with a magic loop.

2 **Round 1:** Using the smaller crochet hook, chain 3, then work 11 double crochet through the loop. Join the last stitch to the beginning of the round by working a slip stitch in the third chain of the beginning chain-3. Pull on the starting yarn to tighten the loop.

3 **Round 2:** Chain 4. Single crochet in the second chain from the hook; half double crochet in the next chain; double crochet in the last chain. This forms a star point.

4 Connect this side of the star point with the center of the star by working a slip stitch in the next double crochet of Round 1. (The first round has 12 stitches, counting the first chain-3, so the points on this star will not be spaced exactly evenly. Just connect each point to the stitch that it falls closest to.)

5 Repeat steps 3 and 4 four times, to make a total of five star points. You will work the last slip stitch in the top of the beginning chain-3 of Round 1, where the first chain-4 of Round 2 starts. Cut the yarn about 4 in. (10 cm) from the hook and pull the end through the loop. Use a yarn needle to weave in the starting and ending tails of yarn.

6 Sew the star onto the wristband. You can also glue it on with fabric glue if you prefer.

You need to know how to: **slip stitch, chain stitch, single crochet, and crochet through the back loops**

Fingerless Mitts

1 Start by making the cuff with color A: Follow steps 1 to 7 for the wristband on pages 116–118.

2 **Round 1:** Join color B in any ridge row on the edge of the cuff by placing a slip knot on the hook then working a slip stitch through the end of one row. Chain 1.

3 Single crochet in the same row that you joined the yarn to. [Chain 1, skip the next flat row, and single crochet in the end of the next ridge row.] Repeat the instructions in brackets all the way around the cuff. At the end, chain 1 and join to the first single crochet with a slip stitch.

4 **Round 2:** Chain 1. Single crochet in every single crochet and chain of the previous round. Fasten off and weave the end of the yarn into the stitches of this round.

5 **Round 3:** Join color C. Single crochet in the same stitch as joining. [Chain 1, skip 1 stitch, single crochet in the next stitch.] Repeat the instructions in brackets around the piece. When you get to the end, chain 1 and join to the beginning of the round by working a slip stitch in the first single crochet. Fasten off and weave in the end.

6 **Round 4:** Join the next color in the stripe pattern (see step 7) in a chain space. Single crochet in the same space as joining. [Chain 1, single crochet in next chain space.] Repeat the instructions in brackets around the piece. When you get to the end, chain 1 and join to the beginning of the round by working a slip stitch in the first single crochet. Fasten off and weave in the end.

7 The stripe pattern for the hand of the fingerless mitt (starting from Round 3) is C, D, A, B. Repeat Round 4 in this stripe pattern until you have two stripes of color A.

8 Now make the hole for the thumb. Join the next color in the pattern (color B) and begin the round as described in step 6. Stop 2 chain spaces from the end. Fasten off and weave in the end.

9 Join the next color at the beginning of the previous row (not where you stopped), and chain 2. Single crochet in the next chain space. [Chain 1, single crochet in the next chain space.] Repeat the instructions in brackets across the row, ending with a single crochet in the last stitch. Fasten off and weave in the end.

10 Join the next color at the beginning of the previous row and single crochet in the beginning chain loop. [Chain 1, single crochet in the next chain space.] Repeat the instructions in brackets across the row, ending with a single crochet in the last stitch. Fasten off and weave in the end.

11 Repeat steps 9 and 10 two more times. Repeat step 9 one more time (you should be on color A) now, but at the end of the row chain 3 and then join them to the beginning of the row with a slip stitch.

12 Continuing in the stripe pattern, work Round 4 four more times, filling in the chain 3 at the end of the thumb with stitches in the pattern. Do not fasten off color A at the end of the last round.

13 Going on with color A, chain 1. Single crochet in each stitch and chain space around. Fasten off and weave in the end. Make the second mitt exactly the same as the first.

TIP

This is another pattern with a lot of ends to weave in! If you don't want to deal with all those ends, you can make it in just one color, and it will still look great. Or you can carry the colors you're not using along the inside of the piece. To do this, when it's time to change colors, don't fasten the old yarn off—just drop it and go on with the new one. Leave the yarn connected to the work, with the end leading to the ball on the inside of the mitt. When you're ready to use that color again, just pull it up *loosely* along the inside of the mitt and start crocheting with it! This will save you some work weaving in ends—but it will only work when you're crocheting in rounds. When you get to the thumb hole you'll have to fasten off the yarn like normal.

Materials

Fingerless Mitts

❀ 2 skeins (1.8 oz./50 g each) medium (weight category 4) wool-acrylic blend yarn in blue (color A)

❀ 1 skein (1.8 oz./50 g) medium (weight category 4) wool-acrylic blend yarn in pink (color B)

❀ 1 skein (1.8 oz./50 g) medium (weight category 4) wool-acrylic blend yarn in mint green (color C)

❀ 1 skein (1.8 oz./50 g) medium (weight category 4) wool-acrylic blend yarn in purple (color D)

❀ U.S. size YY (3.5 mm) crochet hook

❀ Yarn needle

Sweet Cuddly Cat

Crochet a Stuffed Friend

You need to know how to: make a magic loop, chain stitch, slip stitch, single crochet, increase, decrease, half double crochet, double crochet, and sew

You'll learn how to: make a project assembled from many smaller pieces.

Body

1 Start with a magic loop with the blue yarn.

2 **Round 1:** Work 10 single crochets in the magic loop. Join the last stitch to the beginning of the round by working a slip stitch in the third chain of the beginning chain-3. Pull on the starting yarn to tighten the loop.

3 **Round 2:** Continuing around in a spiral, work 2 single crochets in each stitch from the previous round. Mark the beginning of this round (and each round as you continue) with a small piece of yarn in a different color.

4 **Round 3:** Work 1 single crochet in each stitch around.

5 **Round 4:** [Single crochet in the next stitch, then work 2 single crochets in the next stitch.] Repeat the instructions in brackets around the piece.

6 **Round 5:** Same as Round 3.

7 **Round 6:** [Single crochet in the next 2 stitches, then work 2 single crochets in the next stitch.] Repeat the instructions in brackets around the piece.

8 **Round 7:** Same as Round 3.

9 **Round 8:** [Single crochet in the next 3 stitches, then work 2 single crochets in the next stitch.] Repeat the instructions in brackets around the piece.

Materials

- 3 skeins (1.8 oz./50 g each) light (weight category 3) wool-acrylic blend yarn in blue
- 1 skein (3.5 oz/100 g) light (weight category 3) wool-acrylic blend yarn in light pink
- 1 skein (3.5 oz/100 g) light (weight category 3) wool-acrylic blend yarn in bright pink
- Small amount of light (weight category 3) wool-acrylic blend yarn in white
- 6 in. (15 cm) flower wire
- 4 pink buttons, ½ in. (1.5 cm) wide
- 2 black buttons or animal eyes, ¼ in. (8 mm) wide
- Polyester fiberfill
- 4 Tbsp lentils, dried beans, or plastic pellets
- Glue
- U.S. size yy (3.5 mm) crochet hook
- Scissors
- Yarn needle

10 **Rounds 9–27:** Same as Round 3.

11 **Round 28:** [Single crochet in the next 3 stitches, then single crochet 2 together.] Repeat the instructions in brackets around the piece.

12 **Round 29:** Same as Round 3.

13 **Round 30:** [Single crochet in the next 2 stitches, then single crochet 2 together.] Repeat the instructions in brackets around the piece.

14 **Round 31:** Same as Round 3.

15 **Round 32:** [Single crochet in the next stitch, then single crochet 2 together.] Repeat the instructions in brackets around the piece.

16 **Round 33:** Same as Round 3.

17 **Round 34:** Single crochet 2 together. Repeat all the way around the piece. Cut the yarn about 6 in. (15 cm) from the hook and pull the end through the loop.

18 Stuff the cat's body with fiberfill.

19 Use the crochet hook to weave the yarn tail through the stitches of the last round. Pull tight to close up the hole at the end of the body, and tie the yarn off. Weave in the tails of yarn.

Head

1 **Rounds 1–8:** Same as Rounds 1–8 of the body.

2 **Round 9–12:** Single crochet in each stitch around.

3 **Round 13:** [Single crochet in the next 4 stitches, then work 2 single crochets in the next stitch.] Repeat the instructions in brackets around the piece.

4 **Rounds 14–20:** Single crochet in each stitch around.

5 **Round 21:** [Single crochet in the next 4 stitches, then single crochet 2 together.] Repeat the instructions in brackets around the piece.

6 **Round 22:** Single crochet in each stitch around.

7 **Round 23:** [Single crochet in the next 3 stitches, then single crochet 2 together.] Repeat the instructions in brackets around the piece.

8 **Round 24:** Same as Round 22.

9 **Round 25:** [Single crochet in the next 2 stitches, then single crochet 2 together.] Repeat the instructions in brackets around the piece.

10 **Round 26:** Same as Round 22.

11 **Round 27:** [Single crochet in the next stitch, then single crochet 2 together.] Repeat the instructions in brackets around the piece.

12 **Round 28:** Same as Round 22.

13 **Round 29:** Single crochet 2 together. Repeat all the way around the piece. Cut the yarn about 6 in. (15 cm) from the hook and pull the end through the loop.

14 Stuff the head with fiberfill.

15 Use the crochet hook to weave the yarn tail through the stitches of the last round. Pull tight to close up the hole at the end of the body, and tie the yarn off. Weave in the tails of yarn.

Solid-Color Legs

1 Start with a magic loop with the blue yarn.

2 **Round 1:** Work 7 single crochets in the magic loop. Join the last stitch to the beginning of the round by working a slip stitch in the third chain of the beginning chain-3. Pull on the starting yarn to tighten the loop.

3 **Round 2:** Continuing around in a spiral, work 2 single crochets in each stitch from the previous round. Mark the beginning of this round (and each round as you continue) with a small piece of yarn in a different color.

4 **Rounds 3–22:** Single crochet in each stitch around.

5 Use a funnel to put 1 Tablespoon of lentils, dried beans, or plastic pellets into the leg. Add some fiberfill on top of them. Don't put in so much fiberfill that it bulges out—you will want the top part of the leg to be empty.

6 **Round 23:** [Single crochet in the next stitch, then single crochet 2 together.] Repeat the instructions in brackets around the piece.

7 **Round 24:** Single crochet in each stitch around.

8 **Round 25:** Single crochet 2 together. Repeat all the way around the piece. Cut the yarn about 6 in. (15 cm) from the hook and pull the end through the loop.

9 Use the crochet hook to weave the yarn tail through the stitches of the last round. Pull tight to close up the hole at the end of the leg, and tie the yarn off. Weave in the tails of yarn.

10 Repeat steps 1 to 9 to make a second leg.

Two-Color Legs

1 With the light pink yarn, work steps 1 to 3 of the instructions for the solid-color leg.

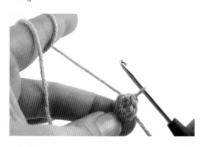

2 **Rounds 3–9:** Single crochet in each stitch around.

3 **Round 10–22:** Join the blue yarn and cut off the pink yarn. Continuing in blue, single crochet in each stitch around for 13 more rounds.

4 Finish the leg as described in steps 5 to 9 of the instructions for the solid-color leg.

5 Repeat these instructions to make a fourth leg, but use bright pink yarn at the beginning instead of light pink.

Tail

1 With the blue yarn, work steps 1 to 3 of the instructions for the solid-color leg.

2 **Rounds 3–9:** Single crochet in each stitch around.

3 **Rounds 10–11:** Join the bright pink yarn and single crochet in each stitch around for 2 rounds. (Don't cut the blue yarn, just keep it on the inside of the piece as you work. You can pick it up when you need it again, with no tails to weave in.)

4 **Rounds 12–13:** Join the light pink yarn (don't cut the bright pink yarn) and single crochet in each stitch around for 2 rounds.

5 **Rounds 14–15:** Pick up the blue yarn from 4 rounds back, pull it up *loosely* on the inside of the tail, and start crocheting with it again. Single crochet in each stitch around for 2 rounds.

6 **Rounds 16–25:** Repeat Rounds 14 and 15 with bright pink, then with light pink, then blue, then bright pink, then light pink. You will have three stripes of both shades of pink.

7 **Rounds 26–31:** Cut both pink yarns and pick up the blue yarn. Single crochet in each stitch around for 6 rounds.

8 Bend the ends of the wire back by about ½ in. (1 cm) at each end. Wrap the wire in fiberfill and push the whole thing into the tail.

9 **Round 32:** [Single crochet in the next stitch, then single crochet 2 together.] Repeat the instructions in brackets around the piece.

10 **Round 33:** Single crochet in each stitch around.

11 **Round 34:** Single crochet 2 together. Repeat all the way around the piece. Cut the yarn about 6 in. (15 cm) from the hook and pull the end through the loop.

12 Use the crochet hook to weave the yarn tail through the stitches of the last round. Pull tight to close up the hole at the end of the leg, and tie the yarn off. Weave in the tails of yarn.

Cheeks

1 Start with a magic loop with the white yarn.

2 **Round 1:** Work 10 single crochets in the magic loop. Join the last stitch to the beginning of the round by working a slip stitch in the third chain of the beginning chain-3. Pull on the starting yarn to tighten the loop.

3 **Round 2:** Single crochet in the first 7 stitches of the previous round. Cut the yarn about 4 in. (10 cm) from the crochet hook and pull the end through the loop. Use a yarn needle to weave in the end.

4 Repeat steps 1 to 3 again to make a second cheek patch.

Nose and Inner Ears

1 With the light pink yarn, chain 6. Half double crochet in the second chain from the hook, half double crochet in the next stitch, work 2 treble crochets in the next stitch, half double crochet in the last 2 stitches.

2 Cut the yarn about 4 in. (10 cm) from the crochet hook and pull the end through the loop. Use a yarn needle to weave in the end.

3 For the inner ears, repeat steps 1 and 2 once more with the light pink yarn and once with the bright pink yarn.

Outer Ears

1 With the blue yarn, chain 9.

2 **Row 1:** Single crochet in the second chain from the hook and in each chain across. Turn.

3 **Row 2:** Chain 1, single crochet in each stitch across until the last 2 stitches, single crochet 2 together in the last 2 stitches. Turn.

4 **Rows 3–8:** Same as Row 2. You should have just 1 stitch left at the end of Row 8. Cut the yarn about 4 in. (10 cm) from the crochet hook and pull the end through the loop. Use a yarn needle to weave in the end.

Assembling and Finishing the Cat

1 Sew or glue the inner ears to the outer ears. Attach the ears, eyes, nose, and cheeks to the cat's head. Sew the tail to the top of the back end of the body.

2 Now work on the legs. Thread the yarn needle with a piece of blue yarn and tie a knot in the end. Insert it through the top end of one leg, then through a button. Send the needle back through another buttonhole and through the leg, then insert the needle into the cat's body where you want the leg to go and bring it out on the opposite side. Stitch through another leg and button from back to front. Stitch back through another buttonhole and back through the leg and the cat's body to where you started. Pull tight to attach the legs firmly to the body. Sew back and forth like this several times, going through all the holes of the buttons. Attach the other pair of legs to the body in the same way.

3 Sew the head to the body. For the whiskers, thread the yarn needle with pink thread and insert it into one cheek and bring it through the head and out the other side. Tie a knot at each end of this length of yarn so it doesn't pull through. Repeat 2 more times. Trim the whiskers to the length you want.

TIP

You can simplify this cat a bit by crocheting all the parts in one color. Or if you like the striped look, you can make it in self-striping yarn for a cat that is patterned over its whole body.

TIP

You can make this pattern into a dog, a sheep, or another four-legged animal with just a few changes. Use a shorter tail, floppy ears (you could make them like the leaves for the garland on page 74), and a button nose to make a dog. Make the body and head from fuzzy white yarn and all the other parts from dark brown or black for a sheep; use floppy ears and a very short tail (or no tail at all).

TIP

As everyone knows, cats don't like water—and this stuffed one is no different! Lentils and dried beans will swell up and sprout if you wash them, so this cat needs to be kept dry if you stuffed its feet with one of those materials. If you want to be able to wash your cat, stuff the feet with plastic pellets.

Visual Index

Franziska Heidenreich

Franziska Heidenreich is the author of eleven craft books for kids and adults. She first got her hands on a crochet hook at the age of seven. No one in her family knew how to crochet, so she taught herself in order to make clothes for her dolls. She has been crocheting ever since. She lives in Berlin with her partner, their son, and their cat.

Thanks to the Coats Company for its support of this book.
Coats GmbH Kensingen
www.schachenmayr.com
www.coatsgmbh.de
We also thank the companies Union Knopf (Bielefeld) and Prym (Stolberg) for providing materials.

Patterns: Franziska Heidenreich
Photos: frechverlag GmbH, 70499 Stuttgart; lichtpunkt, Michael Ruder, Stuttgart
Product Management: Carolin Eichenlaub
Editing: Dr. Christine Schlitt
Interior Design: Katrin Röhlig
Cover Design: Wendy A. Reynolds
Translation: Christine M. Grimm

The original German edition was published as *Häkel mit! — Die Kinderhäkelschule.*
Copyright © 2013 frechverlag GmbH, Stuttgart, Germany (www.frech.de)
This edition is published by arrangement with Claudia Böhme Rights & Literary Agency, Hannover, Germany (www.agency-boehme.com).
Copyright © 2014 by Stackpole Books

Printed in Peoria, IL, by Versa Press in July 2014. Job #J14-03884.

Published by
STACKPOLE BOOKS
5067 Ritter Road
Mechanicsburg, PA 17055
www.stackpolebooks.com

Printed in the United States of America

10 9 8 7 6 5 4 3 2 1

First edition

Library of Congress Cataloging-in-Publication Data
Heidenreich, Franziska.
  [Hakel mit! English]
  Crochet for kids : basic techniques and great projects that kids can make themselves / Franziska Heidenreich.
        pages cm.
  Audience: Ages 7–13.
  ISBN 978-0-8117-1417-4
  1. Crocheting—Juvenile literature.   2. Crocheting—Patterns   I. Title.
  TT820.H44 2014
  746.43'4—dc23
                        2014014846

Crochet from Stackpole Books

CROCHET CRITTERS AND BUGS
22 Great Projects
Edited by Kathryn Fulton
PB, 128 pages, 278 color photos, 7.25 x 9.125, 978-0-8117-1252-1

- Patterns for 25 cute and clever crocheted insects, mollusks, arachnids, and other fun critters
- Hundreds of step-by-step photos illustrate the construction of the projects
- Unique projects including ladybugs, frogs, butterflies, aphids, octopuses, seahorses, horseshoe crabs, jellyfish, slugs, worms, scorpions, dragonflies, and spiders
- Create one-of-a-kind decorations, toys, and gifts

CROCHET WRAPS EVERY WHICH WAY
18 Original Patterns in 6 Techniques
Tammy Hildebrand
PB, 112 pages, 170 color photos, 2 charts, 8 x 10, 978-0-8117-1183-8

- Patterns for 18 wraps and shawls using 6 crochet techniques: traditional crochet, motif crochet, Tunisian crochet, broomstick lace, hairpin lace, and double-ended crochet
- Includes one easy, one intermediate, and one advanced project for each technique
- Accessories for every occasion: delicate shawlettes, comfy ponchos, intricate lace shawls, and vibrant, modern wraps

T-SHIRT YARN
Projects to Crochet and Knit
Sandra Lebrun
PB, 64 pages, 121 color photos, 8.5 x 11, 978-0-8117-1453-2

Yarn made from recycled T-shirt material is quick and easy to work with, in addition to being eco-friendly. This book gives 24 great projects for accessories and home décor using this fun fiber.

- Make fun and stylish purses, hats, scarves, pillows, footstools, baskets, rugs, and more
- Includes 18 crochet projects and 6 knitting projects, all suitable for beginning crafters, plus a step-by-step skills refresher for each technique
- T-shirt yarn yields thick, durable fabric, works up quickly, and creates large, easy-to-see stitches

VINTAGE CROCHET HATS AND ACCESSORIES
23 Classic Hats, Shawls, and Bags
Edited by Kathryn Fulton
PB, 112 pages, 75 color photos, 7.25 x 9.125, 978-0-8117-1447-1

Join in the comeback of the vintage look by making your own hats, handbags, and more in classic styles. These 23 patterns include accessories for women, men, and children, all with a vintage-chic look.

- 23 patterns for hats, purses and tote bags, shawls, and more
- All the patterns have been fully tested and edited to appeal to a contemporary audience; terminology and yarn information have been updated
- Styles for all tastes and ages
- Patterns range from easy to experienced

Leading the Way in Crafts

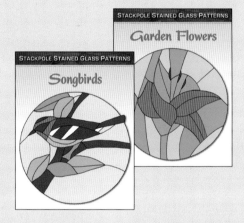